# Multi-Sensory Scripture

MULTI-SENSORY SCRIPTURE by Sue Wallace

Scripture Union, 207–209 Queensway, Bletchley, MK2 2EB, UK
e-mail: info@scriptureunion.org.uk
www.scriptureunion.org.uk

Scripture Union Australia: Locked Bag 2, Central Coast Business Centre, NSW 2252
www.su.org.au

ISBN 1 84427 166 8
First published in Great Britain by Scripture Union 2005
© Sue Wallace

Cover design by waldonwhitejones of Basildon, Essex, UK

Internal illustrations by Fred Chevalier

Internal page design by Creative Pages: www.creativepages.co.uk

Printed and bound in Malta by Interprint Limited

Scripture Union is an international Christian charity working with churches in more than 130 countries providing resources to bring the good news about Jesus Christ to children, young people and families – and to encourage them to develop spiritually through the Bible and prayer. As well as a network of volunteers, staff and associates who run holidays, church-based events and school Christian groups, Scripture Union produces a wide range of publications and supports those who use their resources through training programmes.

# Multi-Sensory Scripture

50 innovative ideas for exploring the Bible
in churches and small groups

Sue Wallace

# Thanks

Firstly, I'd like to thank God, who constantly amazes and surprises me with new gifts each day. Next, I'd like to thank the Visions community, who support me in so many practical ways; and the shipmates from the Ship of Fools message boards, who kindly let me pick their brains. Thanks to Malcolm Wallace, for just being brilliant; to the IBVM for encouraging me to read the Bible when I was young; to Sharon Stinson, for continuing to show us new things. Thanks to Anne Gray, for being a great cook; to Jonny Baker, Grace, Resonance, Revive and the other creative groups who work so hard at bringing new worship to birth; to Bishop Graham Cray for getting us off the ground in the first place. Thanks to Roger, Ian and the staff of St Michael le Belfrey for their constant support, and all the great people I'm getting to get to know at NOC. I am really grateful to all of you – and to the people I'm sure I've forgotten to whom I owe so much!

Sue Wallace

# Contents

**Note**: Many of these activities come with a ready-to-use script set out so that you can easily photocopy it and distribute it to readers. But remember that these scripts could be used in other ways, such as pre-recorded, or as PowerPoint or OHP presentations with appropriate images.

# Introduction from the author

The Bible is life-giving and life-changing! As we explore it with creativity and imagination which touch all the senses, we release it to richly impact our lives. The Bible and our response to it is the focus of this book and all the creative activities in it. Almost all have been tried, tested and improved by real experiences in congregational and small group settings.

The inspiration for many of the ideas in *Multi-Sensory Scripture* has come through Visions, a weekly multimedia worship service attached to St Michael le Belfrey Church in York, where our aim is to use art and creativity to help us pray, worship and learn more about how to follow Christ. I have also gained inspiration from other creative worship groups around the country, Christian friends I have met on the web, Orthodox Christians, Catholic prayer groups and other staff members of St Michael's who make our early morning staff prayer meetings so innovative week by week.

My encouragement to readers and users of *Multi-Sensory Scripture* and the two companion books I have written in the series – *Multi-Sensory Church* and *Multi-Sensory Prayer* – is to feel free to experiment, change and adapt the ideas to suit your own church situation. If one of the ideas leads you to doing something totally new instead, then so much the better!

Sue Wallace

# 1  Scarlet and snow

This idea works best with small groups, although you can use it with larger numbers of people as long as they are all able to see what's happening easily. It is a very creative way of confessing our sins to God together and brings the theme of the 'scarlet and snow' verse (Isaiah 1:18) home in a very vivid way.

## Resources
You will need: pieces of red paper or card; some larger sheets of paper (newspaper will do); pencils; talcum powder (preferably baby powder).

## Method
Place the large pieces of paper in the centre of your group on the floor, and lay the pieces of red paper or card on top. Then read **The scarlet and snow script** (page 36).

# 2  Dissolving

(with thanks to Clare Rishbeth)

## Resources
You will need: a clear bowl filled with water (or several bowls if it's a big group; large Pyrex ones are great); a kneeler or cushion; some sterilising tablets (large tablets such as Milton work best) or soluble vitamin tablets; pencils. An optional extra would be a wooden or paper cross hanging on the wall or in the space above the bowls, or an enlarged printout of Isaiah 1:18 or other verses about forgiveness. IMPORTANT – These tablets do release a small amount of chlorine gas, so always use them in a well-ventilated area. If in doubt about ventilation, or with younger age groups, opt for the vitamin tablets instead.

## Method
Fill the bowl or bowls with water and place where they can be easily seen; put the cushion or kneeler beside it. Then hand out the tablets and pencils to your group. If you have a large group or a whole congregation, it may still be possible to do this by sharing the sterilising or vitamin tablets in twos or threes as you pass them around.

Then invite your group to write whatever sins or hurts they wish to on the tablets. Obviously there is limited space on the tablets, so encourage them to use just initials or symbols that are just between them and God to represent their words. If you are sharing, remember that you can use both sides of the tablets.

Allow time for everyone to write on the tablets; then invite anyone who wants to, to come and kneel beside the bowl and drop the tablets in. As they do so, they can ask God to forgive their sins.

Leave plenty of space for the congregation or group just to watch the tablets dissolve. You may like to play a song about forgiveness as this is happening, or a piece of instrumental music. In a few minutes – as long as too many tablets aren't dropped into the same bowl – the tablets will dissolve completely, leaving no trace that they were ever there; a poignant symbol of the extent of God's forgiveness. You might like to read Titus 3:3–7 to conclude.

## Variation
An additional or alternative activity is to get people to write on the tablets anything that is a barrier to them worshipping God – for example, worries, stresses or fears.

# 3  Wiping the slate clean

(with thanks to Helen Turner)

This is a symbolic action confession shown to me by Helen Turner. We used it one Good Friday as one of the installations we put in our local Christian cafe to help people pray.

### Resources

You will need: a collection of slates (we used drinks coasters made of slate, but you could also use small pieces of wood covered in blackboard paint); chalk; a bowl or bucket; a wet cloth.

### Method

Hand around the slates and pieces of chalk. If you have not got enough slates for everyone, you can appoint some people to collect the slates once they have been wiped, to re-use for someone else. Alternatively, you can set everything up as an installation so that not everyone visits the station at once and you have a chance to re-use the slates. When we did this, we placed our bowl at the foot of a large cross.

Ask people to write down anything that they wish to apologise to God for: specific sins; grudges against other people; things they find it hard to forgive and forget. Then invite them to come up and wipe their slate clean. During this time, you can read out a Bible passage about God's forgiveness, such as Titus 3:3–7 or Psalm 32.

### Variation

This prayer action is also very effective as an action of reconciliation between people or groups who have had disagreements in the past and want to put those arguments behind them. In this scenario, you may wish to have a large blackboard for everyone to write on. After the writing about the past sins has been washed away, you can replace it by writing words of encouragement and prayers of mutual support.

# 4 Sackcloth bands

Sackcloth is used in many places in the Bible as a sign of repentance. This activity is a way of using sackcloth in a creative way, almost like a friendship band, as an aid to our prayers for our cities, towns and villages, and for our society.

### Resources

You will need: strips of hessian (enough for one each) two or three centimetres wide, long enough to wrap and tie around the average wrist; ballpoint pens; ashes (optional). You can get ashes from some Christian bookshops or make your own in advance by burning some wood, but be aware of fire safety. Ensure the ashes are completely cool before using them.

### Method

Give a strip of hessian and a pen to each person in your group or congregation. Read Daniel 9:1–11;17–19. Mention the fact that here Daniel is apologising on behalf of others. He is crying to God for forgiveness on behalf of the Jewish people, even though he himself has tried to follow God's laws. This is a time for us to do the same. Invite people to write prayers of repentance, or just name things that their community or nation has done that they wish to say sorry to God for. Invite God to forgive, heal and help. If you wish, you can then sprinkle ashes on the strips of cloth. Tie the strips into bracelets and wear as a reminder to keep praying for all those situations.

# 5 Sand confession

(by Sophie Dutton, used by permission)

This confession was originally written for some prayer installations for a youth event. It's particularly appropriate to use as an installation, but could be used in a group setting or for a service led from the front as long as you have access to enough trays of sand. Of course, those of you fortunate enough to be living near to a beach might decide that an outdoor event would be really great!

## Resources

You will need: trays of sand; tealight candles; a metal tray; a second tray or candle stand; the script – either printed on paper and distributed, or recorded on a tape, or led by a good reader.

## Method

This script is loosely based on John 8:1–11. Depending on your time constraints and how well you feel your group knows the Bible passage, you might want to read it out first. Then hand out, read or play **The confession script** (page 37).

# 6 The dirty mirror

This is a prayer of preparation for worship, based on verses from the Sermon on the Mount (Matthew 5–7). Although it works best with a small group, it can be used in a larger gathering as long as everyone can see the mirror.

## Resources

You will need: a candle (a large fat candle works best; remember to position it safely); a mirror or mirror tile (again, be careful that it is placed where it cannot slip and break); a lipstick (preferably a strong dark colour); a cloth; a bottle of glass cleaner.

## Method

Explain that we are going to have a time of prayer and preparation for worship. Light the candle and place the mirror where it reflects the light of the candle. (It is a good idea to experiment beforehand for the best place so that most people can see what is happening). Then read **The mirror script** (page 38).

# 7 Litter

This can be a very powerful way of saying sorry to God, and of clearing away the clutter that gets in the way of our relationship with him.

## Resources

You will need: a collection of litter. This needs to be nice, clean litter – nothing too messy or difficult to clean up! Choose things like empty paper and cardboard packets, cigarette boxes, junk mail, small plastic drinks bottles (sealed), till receipts, sweet packets. Make sure there is at least enough for one piece of litter per person. Also: biros or felt-tips (or you could use OHP pens if you need to write on plastic); a volunteer with a large broom. (You could have your volunteer dressed in a white coat or overalls to be more dramatic.) Also: music to play (optional).

## Advance preparation

Before you do this symbolic action, have a practice with your litter and your broom in the venue you are going to use, just to check that the broom *can* sweep everything away successfully.

## Method

Place the litter at various points around the room or church hall, making sure that it's all accessible. Ask each person to choose and go to stand by a piece of litter that they feel represents them and their lives in some way. Then ask them to think and pray for a while about the junk in their lives. What things do they need to apologise to God for, so that they can begin again? What things get in the way of their relationship with God? For example: worries… time constraints… the phone ringing… fears… doubts… work stress.

Give time for people to think about these things. Perhaps play an appropriate piece of music. Then ask everyone to put their name on their piece of junk. If they wish to, they can add words or symbols for the things in their lives they want God to get rid of. Finally, ask everyone to put their pieces of junk on the floor at a point indicated by you (one that is easy to sweep, based on your experiments earlier). Symbolically, the best place is likely to be the aisle or somewhere central. Ask the group or congregation to contemplate the rubbish for a moment. Then read Isaiah 11:15 – 12:2 as everyone watches the volunteer sweep all the rubbish away.

# 8 Thistles

We often think about the good seed in the Parable of the Sower, but frequently ignore the weeds and thistles – and this is where the focus is for this creative confession and Bible meditation.

### Resources

You will need: a collection of thistledown or burrs (preferably enough so that each person can have some); a barbecue; some kindling; matches; other seeds (sunflower seeds or nuts are ideal). This is an activity where you will need to be mindful of safety. It's better to place the barbecue outside in a place sheltered from the wind – otherwise you might end up planting thistles in the church garden!

### Method

Begin by reading the Parable of the Sower in Matthew 13:3–9,18–23, and the Parable of the Weeds in Matthew 13:24–29; then appoint a good reader to read **The thistles script** (page 39).

# 9 Scripture news

It can be an incredibly powerful experience to interweave a Bible reading with current events going on in the world, especially if the reading is chosen carefully. This was especially true of those in our church in York on the Sunday following the day which has now forever become known as 9/11. That Sunday we threw out our service plan and started from scratch, having a service of mourning and prayer for the victims caught up in the World Trade Center tragedy.

Sometimes even the assigned reading in your regular devotional material or your pattern of services can be incredibly poignant when mixed with news items.

### Resources

You will need: two or three good readers; a Bible; either a newspaper or notes from various news broadcasts and/or websites.

### Method

Think and a pray about some of the news items that have been particularly prominent this week. Then select a Bible reading to compare and contrast with those stories, or pick news items that seem to relate to the current Bible reading for that week.

For example, with a Bible reading about repentance such as Psalm 51, you could choose some of the offences and transgressions of our society to put against the reading. With a more upbeat Bible reading you may wish to put headlines or quotes that provide us with reasons to be thankful.

Divide the Bible verses so that there are a couple of lines of Bible text alternating with a couple of lines of news. Have one person read the Bible extract and another person (or people) read the news extracts. You may want to leave space at the end for silent prayer, or play a piece of music so that people have a chance to reflect on the things they have heard.

Here is an example – in fact, the one we wrote for our 9/11 service. In this case the Bible reading (extracts from Jeremiah 4:22–26) was interspersed with actual quotations from individuals caught up in the tragedy. I find it moves me even now. As you read **The scripture news script** (page 40), you might like to pray for those who are still suffering the aftermath of this tragedy, after all this time. You can use it as a model for a script using different news items.

# 10 Light cubes

We first used this as an installation for a Good Friday service when very young children were present and we didn't want to expose them to fire hazards from candles. The cubes have a similar symbolism to candles but are much safer and cool to the touch.

## Resources

You will need: light cubes – these are like ice cubes but made of plastic and designed to be frozen and placed in drinks. To light them, you just tap their base sharply. You can get them from Marks and Spencer home departments, order them on the Internet or buy them from some trendy gadget shops. Also: a tall clear glass vase (or vases) of water; some acetate or cellophane (this can be coloured if you wish, and is available cheaply from art shops); acetate pens or felt-tips (acetate pens are preferable; the felt-tips will smudge if you are not careful); clear sticky tape.

## Method

Measure a piece of acetate or cellophane to go around your vase or vases and cut to fit but do not attach. Pass the sheet around so that people can write their prayers on it. You might want to encourage them to pray particularly for those in prison, those who are bruised and those who are sitting in darkness – either literal darkness or the darkness of depression or grief.

When everyone has written on the sheet, tape it around your vase of water and then invite people to light the cubes and drop them into the vase. While people are lighting the cubes you can read Isaiah 42:1–7 or another scripture passage about darkness and light. You could use two clear vases, placing them either side of a communion table instead of the usual candles; or you could position the vases at strategic points around the room or space, particularly if you feel some people would be inhibited about going to the front or to one prominent position.

The light of the cubes will shine through the cellophane and light up people's prayers in a rather beautiful way.

## Variation

You can use Christmas lights inside the vase instead of cubes. Obviously, if you do this you must not put any water inside the vase but make sure that the inside is perfectly dry.

# 11 The plumb line

This is an activity to help us bring news events before God in prayer. It is also an opportunity to thank God for the righteous actions of those doing the right things, often in difficult circumstances, and to pray for mercy and help for those suffering injustice.

## Resources

You will need: a plumb line. The simplest way to make this is to tie a weight on a length of string and hang it from a secure fixing in the roof or ceiling, or from a nail above a doorway until it comes to rest. The small weight from a pressure cooker works very well. Make sure that the string is long enough for the weight to be fairly near the ground – that way there's no chance of it falling on someone's head! Also: newspapers; magazines; missionary news updates; pegs or paper clips. The ideal pegs are those miniature plastic pegs used to hang up Christmas cards.

## Method

Appoint a good reader to read **The plumb line script** (page 41).

# 12 Scrapping injustice

Sometimes it's appropriate to get angry about the injustice in the world. Jesus certainly got angry about the temple money changers; and the Psalms are full of a whole range of emotions, including anger. This activity is a way of turning some of our anger about injustice into prayer, as well as a way of celebrating our hope that one day all pain, sorrow, fear and death will be binned, never to be seen again!

**Resources**

You will need a bin (a small household wastepaper bin is fine); paper; pencils.

**Method**

Make sure that everyone has a piece of paper and a pencil and that the bin is placed at a focal point in the space. Then read some or all of the Bible passages on the script, interspersed with current examples of news or statistics from different countries. You might wish to use some information from charities as well.

Some useful websites offering this kind of information:

**www.amnesty.org      www.barnabasfund.org      www.24-7prayer.com**

Don't be afraid to speak the Bible verses and the facts out in a forceful voice as you present **The scrapping injustice script** (page 42).

# 13  Swords into ploughshares

(with thanks to Fusilli from the Ship of Fools community)

This is a creative way of praying for situations of conflict in the world while having Isaiah's prophecy about peace at the forefront of our minds to offer us hope and inspiration.

**Resources**

You will need: a sheet of tinfoil, pre-cut into small squares; a large map of the world (or the particular area of the world you have decided to concentrate on); current news items. You can resource extra information on the websites mentioned in activity 12; also, you can log onto the websites of any other missionary organisations you know. Try to ensure that even less well-known conflicts are included.

**Method**

Place the map in the centre of the group or the space you are using, on the floor or on a large table or pinned on a large board, and read **The swords into ploughshares script** (page 44).

# 14  Wallet prayers

This is a great way of praying for how we use our money and for people in positions of responsibility or power. Sometimes we forget about many of these people, only remembering the politicians who hit the headlines regularly. This method of prayer helps us remember many of the less well-known people who also help our daily lives run smoothly.

**Resources**

No special resources are needed apart from people's own wallets or purses, but you may wish to warn your group in advance to make sure they bring them.

**Method**

Read 1 Timothy 2:1–8, then explain that we are going to use our wallets and purses as aids in prayer. Invite the congregation or group to open and look at their wallets. Families can all look at one person's wallet or purse and pray together. Then read **The wallet prayers script** (page 45) pausing where appropriate.

# 15  Bread prayers

(with thanks to Anne Gray for the recipe)

Communion is the ultimate multi-sensory worship and Bible experience. Simply using bread and wine takes us to the foot of the cross itself. As Paul says, *For whenever you eat this bread and drink this cup, you proclaim the Lord's death until he comes* (1 Corinthians 11:26). For this reason we often like to bring our prayers to the communion table in a creative way. In this activity our prayers are actually baked into the bread.

In my companion book *Multi-Sensory Church* (9 Bread and Wine) I have included a recipe for naan bread and a method of making it as part of a service. Here we have devised a recipe for gluten-free naan bread which means that those with coeliac disease can take full part in communion.

### Resources

You will need: a portable grill or stove – something to grill or fry the bread on. Please think carefully about fire safety and make sure that the grill is in a safe place, well away from children and flammable items. Also: a baking tray; a bottle of wine or grape juice; the usual cups and plates needed for communion.

## Anne's gluten-free and dairy-free naan bread recipe

This will make 2 large naan breads:

| | |
|---|---|
| 8 oz gluten-free flour | 1 teaspoon sugar |
| 2 teaspoons xanthan gum | 1 teaspoon dried yeast |
| (optional, prevents the bread being too flat and cardboard-like; you can buy this from health food shops) | 5 fluid oz warm water |
| | A knob of dairy-free margarine |
| half teaspoon salt | foil |

Please note that this dough is not like ordinary bread dough. It doesn't hold itself together. This is why you put it on foil to cook under the grill.

### Method

**1** Before you begin the service (this needs to be about an hour before you want to do the prayer activity) add sugar to warm water and sprinkle on yeast; wait until frothy. Mix other bread ingredients together and stir into the frothy yeast liquid, adding more warm water if necessary to make a soft dough. Cover and leave to rise until roughly doubled in size (half to one hour depending on how warm it is!)

**2** Five minutes before you reach the part of the service where you want to do this activity, preheat the grill on high. Grease a piece of foil about 30 x 20cm, then take half the dough and roll or pat out onto the foil to a naan bread shape (about 0.75 to 1cm thick).

**3** An important part of the naan bread recipe is that it needs to be pricked before cooking. This is the time when people have the opportunity to add their own prayers to the loaf. When you are nearly ready to grill or fry the naan bread, hand the bread around with a fork or skewer so that anyone who wishes to, can mark the initials of someone they wish to pray for, or a country's initials or a symbol that describes their prayer, using a fork on the dough.

Make sure that you leave enough time to cook the bread and cool it so as not to burn the minister's hands before the communion prayer starts!

**4** Brush the bread with a little oil. Then grill or turn into a frying pan to fry till brown. Turn over and prick, brush with oil and grill or fry the second side. You can repeat with the other half of the dough if you wish, or use that as a practice loaf before the service. Alternatively, you could have two grills or frying pans available so that you can do two loaves at once.

After the bread has been cooked, continue with the communion prayer according to the normal custom in your church.

# 16  Boats

This idea works very well as a prayerful response to the meditation on the calming of the storm (Mark 4:35–41). It is a way of turning the passage into intercession for ourselves and our world – and the boats look great! We also found that grown-ups liked to play with the boats during coffee at the end of the service just as much as the children, creating storms by blowing and then waiting for the pool to calm.

### Resources
You will need: a large paddling pool with a thin layer of water; A4 pieces of paper; pens or pencils. Additionally, you might like to put a large candle, tall enough in its candlestick to stand far out of the water, into the middle of the pool.

### Method
Give out paper and pens and invite people to write prayers for any who are going through stormy times at the moment. Then show them how to turn their pieces of paper into origami boats (see instructions) and float them on the pool. It's a good idea to teach a couple of your church members how to make the boats in advance so that they can help any who get stuck. You might think everyone would know how to make a paper boat, but I've discovered this is not actually the case!

To make a simple origami boat, following the illustrations:

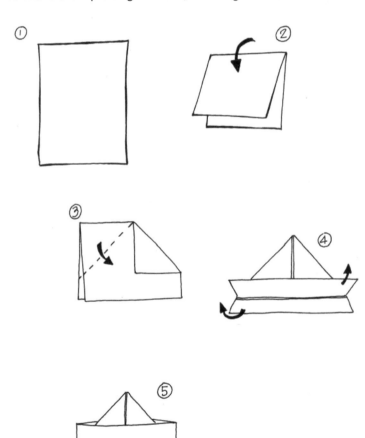

1   take a piece of paper;

2   fold in half;

3   fold two corners down from the folded edge;

4   fold up either side from the open edges at the bottom;

5   put your fingers up inside to open the shape out a little so that it will float.

### Variation
If time is limited, you can make boats in advance and then get people to write their prayers on them using key words or symbols.

# 17  Labels

We did this as a prayer response to a passage in Acts 10, in which Peter has a vision which tells him not to call anything unclean that God has called clean. We found that this time of prayer was a very appropriate preparation for communion.

## Resources

You will need: a piece of material (such as a sheet) made into a hammock; some string to tie the hammock up; some toy animals or sculptures of animals; some luggage labels and pens. (Buying luggage labels can be quite expensive but it's easy to make your own. Cut rectangles of card, punch a hole at one end and thread a short length of string through.) Also: a cross with arms thin enough to attach the labels to.

## Method

String the hammock between two suitably strong points in your church, near the front where everyone can see it. It's a good idea to keep the hammock low enough so that everyone can reach. Place the animals in the hammock. This is most effective if you make sure you have a selection of 'unclean' animals. (See Leviticus 11 for ideas.)

Appoint a good reader to read Acts 10:9–16. Give out the luggage labels and pens and ask everyone to think about some negative 'labels' others have used against them, or that they have used against other people. You can think of some examples, such as 'fat', 'lazy', 'ugly', 'thick', 'useless', 'tart', 'dippy' and so on. Obviously, be careful with your choice of examples – you don't want to upset anyone.

Then invite members of the congregation or group to bring the labels to the front and place them on one of the animals. Later in the service or meeting ask each person who brought a label to come to the front and take another label back to their space. Then have a time of quiet prayer for people who have to put up with being called these things. You might like to pass the labels around while you are doing this, so that more people are prayed for.

When everyone has had a chance to pray, bring the labels up to the cross, and tie them around it. Then, read the following Bible verses to conclude:

> *Surely he took up our infirmities*
> *and carried our sorrows,*
> *yet we considered him stricken by God,*
> *smitten by him, and afflicted.*
> *But he was pierced for our transgressions,*
> *he was crushed for our iniquities;*
> *the punishment that brought us peace was upon him,*
> *and by his wounds we are healed.*
>
> Isaiah 53:4,5

# 18  Broken hearts

We first did this prayer activity at a communion service during the Greenbelt festival, discovering that following it with communion was an incredibly moving experience. Also, because our communion table was made of glass and we were lighting the table from beneath, the hearts glowed and even shone on the ceiling in a very beautiful way.

## Resources

You will need: red tissue paper or glassine paper (similar to tissue but waxed) cut into enough squares for everyone to have one; pencils, biros or felt-tip pens; a communion table (we made ours out of a sheet of perspex resting on large boxes; a projector or desk lamp (optional).

## Method

Give everyone a piece of red paper at least A5 size and a pencil or pen. Explain that we are going to make hearts. It is important that people know in advance that their paper hearts are going to be broken, or they may be sad about their artwork being torn. Ask everyone to create heart shapes. The easiest way to do this is to fold the paper in two and tear half a heart out, which when opened becomes a whole heart. Next ask everyone to tear their heart in two to create a broken heart. At this point they might like to swap their heart with one of their neighbours.

Next, give everyone the chance to write on their hearts the names of broken-hearted people, countries or situations that come to mind. They might like to remember victims of war, the bereaved, those who have lost their will to live, those who are suffering illness, the unemployed etc.

Then, invite everyone to come to the table and place their broken hearts on it as a sign of offering those situations to Jesus, whose blood was poured out for our forgiveness and healing on the cross. While people are doing this, read Psalm 22:14–22.

Then, if you are using a perspex or glass table, switch the lamp or projector on beneath the table. The light will shine up through the hearts making a wonderful glow and lighting up the entire table.

The perfect way to finish these prayers for the broken-hearted is to lay the table with bread and wine and have communion.

# 19  Pipe cleaners

(with thanks to Sophie Dutton)

One of our favourite recent discoveries for alternative worship services in York has been the usefulness and versatility of pipe cleaners! We have used them for creative intercessions on a number of occasions, but they are versatile enough to use for teaching or creative interpretation of Bible passages as well.

### Resources

You will need: a collection of pipe cleaners (preferably coloured). These are easily available from stationary and craft shops. They come in small and large sizes, but we find the larger ones are more versatile. Also: large pieces of paper cut into the shape of hands or alternatively the silhouette of hands projected onto a screen.

### Method

Give out the pipe cleaners at the start of the service or time of intercession. Ask everyone to make a symbol or initial of some world situation that they want to place in God's hands at this time. If you have enough pipe cleaners, people can make symbols for a number of situations. Ask people to bring their pipe cleaner creations to the front and place them on the paper hands or beneath the image of the hands, imagining that they are placing these world situations into God's hands. Finish the time of intercession by reading the following verses:

> Shout for joy, O heavens;
>> rejoice, O earth;
>> burst into song, O mountains!
> For the LORD comforts his people
>> and will have compassion on his afflicted ones.
> But Zion said, 'The LORD has forsaken me,
>> the LORD has forgotten me.'
> 'Can a mother forget the baby at her breast
>> and have no compassion on the child she has borne?
> Though she may forget,
> I will not forget you!
> See, I have engraved you on the palms of my hands...'

Isaiah 49:13–16

## Variation

A variation on this technique is to use pipe cleaners to creatively interpret a Bible passage. One example would be the passage about the Church being different parts of a body (1 Corinthians 12:12–31). Each person could sculpt their pipe cleaner into the body part that they feel they are in relation to the church at that moment. You could then discuss and pray about the parts that seem to be missing, and also use the sculptures as inspiration to pray for opportunities to use everyone's gifts and talents.

# 20 Psalm consequences

(adapted from an idea by Paul Millard)

The first time I came across this idea was when Paul Millard led our church staff prayers one morning. I loved the way the consequences structure gave everyone a chance to write prayers of praise and worship to God and how the more poetic people could help the less confident writers produce wonderful pieces of poetry and prayer. This idea can be done with a group of people of any size.

## Resources

You will need: a piece of A4 paper, a pen and a Bible for each person; perhaps a CD player and some music.

## Method

Choose a couple of praise psalms to read to inspire you in your prayers as a group. Good examples are Psalm 92, Psalm 95:1–7 or Psalm 148. Share in the reading, going around the group reading two verses of the psalm each.

Give out the paper and pens and explain that we are going to create our own psalm of praise to God in a similar manner to the consequences game.

Ask everyone to fold their pieces of paper into eight vertical sections and unfold them so that the creases can be seen. Then ask the group to:

1  Write at the top an address of praise to God, for example: 'Lord, I worship you'.

2  Ask everyone to fold their first piece over backwards so the words can't be seen and then pass their piece of paper to the person on their left.

3  On the next section write an aspect of God's character starting with 'because' – for example, 'because you are good'. Fold and pass once more.

4  Then write another aspect of God's character starting with 'and'. Fold and pass again.

5  Now write two things about how wonderful God's creation is, such as, 'Your mountains are big, your rivers shine in the sun'. Fold and pass again.

6  Write something God does for you personally. It could be something like 'You guide me'. Fold and pass.

7  Write a  personal message to Jesus with 'because' in the middle, for example: 'I thank you, Jesus, because you died for me'. Fold and pass again.

8  Write a resolution, such as, 'Therefore I will be glad and share your love with others'.

Fold and pass one final time.

Finally, open out the pieces of paper and read the results out loud, perhaps over some instrumental music.

To encourage you about how creative the results can be, here is an example that our home group came up with:

> *O God, you are more powerful than the wicked men of earth.*
> *You are the source of all our joy and wonder and beauty;*

*And love is your middle name.*
*Your mountains rise to greet the dawn, the seas roar at your sunrise;*
*You reveal yourself in ways that surprise us.*
*Jesus, you are cool, because you didn't just tell us the way, you showed us!*
*Therefore, I will praise and worship you forever! Amen.*

# 21  A dramatic meal

The inspiration for this idea probably came from those murder mystery kits that you can buy for dinner parties. It is best done in a small group situation where you can interact with the other characters properly. Of course, there is nothing to stop you having a large room full of small groups at different tables, with each table having their own meal at the same time. The idea behind the dramatic meal is that instead of having a character briefing for a murder mystery, you have a character briefing for a meal with some of the characters in a Bible story at the table. If you wish to, you can dress to suit your character, but that's entirely optional. However, it does help you get into role.

The most important thing, though, is that you need to hold the entire conversation at the table as if you were the character you are given.

## Resources

You will need: a meal – not absolutely essential, but does make the atmosphere less nervous for those not used to doing drama. It could simply be a matter of having some 'biblical' ingredients on your table, such as bread, fried fish, olives, figs and wine or grape juice. Also: typed character briefings. (It is a good idea to give these out in advance, so that people can think and read up on their character if they wish to.) Also: a Bible and concordance just in case people need to look something up. Optional extras would be simple props which help people get into role. These could be oddments of material, coloured headscarves, a few bits of jewellery, walking sticks, hats etc.

## Method

Ahead of time, decide simple housekeeping issues such as where you are going to hold your meal and what foods you need to prepare for it. Don't forget to check people's special dietary requirements.

Choose a Bible passage. Some of the passages from the Gospels work particularly well, but be more creative if your group has some experience of drama. Write your character briefings and decide at what point in the narrative the meal is taking place. For example, if your passage is the calming of the storm, you might assume that the meal is taking place on the evening following the storm.

Either allocate your characters or let people choose their character. Some people might be happy to have a major talking role, others to merely listen most of the time. Give everyone a week or so to do any homework they'd like to do; then enjoy your meal!

We've discovered that it's important to have a debriefing time after the meal, when people can step out of role and describe what they gained from the experience.

As an example, you will find **The Lazarus meal**, complete with character briefings, on page 68.

# 22  Trinity hand symbol

This activity has been inspired by the Orthodox tradition. The hand position is used by Orthodox Christians when they make the sign of the cross.

## Resources

No special resources are needed for this except the script and a couple of people willing to demonstrate.

You might like to play some gentle music behind the Scripture verses in **The Trinity script** (page 48).

# 23 Family tree

One of the things I like about this idea is that it uses a part of the Bible that people tend to skip over – the part some call 'the begats'. The activity helps us thank God for all those people who have helped us get to know him.

### Resources

You will need: photocopies of the tree outline (page 46) one for each person; Bibles; a concordance; pencils or pens; green felt-tip pens.

### Method

Read Matthew1:1–16 together. If you are in a small group situation, you may wish to chat about some of the names that are more familiar from that list, reminding each other of who's who. If you are in a church service situation, you may wish to talk about the famous names who come into this list. Having a concordance may come in handy if you are in a small group, to look up where these names are mentioned in other parts of the Bible. Read **The family tree script** (page 47).

# 24 Chewing things over

I was originally taught this method of reading the Bible at school. I've been very glad that I was given this as a tool because at times, when I have been unable to concentrate on studying because of illness or other reasons, I have been able to 'chew over' verses that I knew by heart as well as being able to use it to turn my Bible reading into prayer. You can use this method to 'chew over' passages in a group, but you need to find a way in which you can all work undisturbed and at your own pace. One way of achieving this would be to have it as an installation or as one choice among a number of activities.

### Resources

You will need: nothing special apart from a Bible.

### Method

This technique can be used for many parts of the Bible, but it works best with some of the deeper passages. Christ's words in the Gospels, especially John's Gospel, are very good for this, as are parts of the Psalms. Pick passages that are not too long. For this example, I am going to choose part of John 15:5: *I am the vine; you are the branches.*

Make yourself comfortable so that you can think and pray undisturbed. You might want to play some gentle music, or to lie or kneel down, but you don't need to do any of these things as long as you are in a place where you will not be distracted.

Read your short passage or verse once through, perhaps reading a bit of the section around it to get the context, so that the passage's meaning is not distorted. Then pray that God will speak to you through these words of Scripture.

Then begin to 'chew over' the words of your text, just one or two at a time. Below is an example of the sort of things you might think about, but it is just one example. The next time you think about these same words, your thoughts might go in a completely different direction.

> *I am* … what does that phrase mean? Constancy… dependability… unchangeableness... being there for me… What does it remind me of? Are there other places in the Bible where that phrase has been used? Yes… the burning bush… Moses… God saying to Moses, when he asked his name, 'I am who I am'… past and future… I was… I will be… constant care… constant love.

*... the vine* ... What do vines make me think of? Fruit! Delicious grapes... refreshing new wine... communion... being joined to God and one another... What does the vine itself remind me of? Plants growing... nourishment being carried by the sap... being fed by the roots... being watered.

*... you are* ... a statement of existence... I exist because God exists... I have life... and Jesus has promised that would be eternal life... *whoever lives and believes in me will never die* (John 11:26).

*... the branches* ... a statement of belonging... I am part of that vine... Others are part of that vine... on different branches... They look like they are growing in different directions – but they are connected to the same vine... The branches bear leaves... they are green and growing all the time ... the branches sometimes bear fruit... Maybe I can pray for more growth... more fruit.

When you have finished 'chewing over' your verse or passage, thank God for any new things he has shown you through it.

# 25 Connections web

This is a creative way of looking at the 'bigger picture' of the Bible, rather than at individual stories on their own. It is best done with groups who already have a fairly good knowledge of the Bible as it relies on using that knowledge to forge connections. It can lead to some very interesting discussions, as people make connections that others may find surprising or haven't seen before.

### Resources

You will need: a collection of pieces of card with the names of Bible characters written on them; string, tape or lengths of wool; Blu-Tack or pins; some kind of large board; small pieces of paper or post-it notes; Bibles; concordances.

### Method

In advance, write the names of Bible characters on the pieces of card. Choose any you wish, but here are some examples you could use: Adam / Eve / Abraham / Isaac / Moses / Hannah / Elkanah / David / Elijah / Elizabeth / Zechariah / Paul / the angel Gabriel / Joseph / Peter / The woman caught in adultery / John the Baptist.

In some cases where names could refer to more than one character, you will need to add a Bible reference so that people are sure which one is intended, eg Joseph (Genesis 40) would make sure that this Joseph wasn't mixed up with Mary's husband.

You can also provide blank cards so that people can add other names during the activity.

Spread the cards over a table, the ground or pin them onto a board or wall. Then invite people to post 'connections' on the display. For example, someone might put a piece of tape between Elizabeth and Hannah, saying that they both gave birth to prophets. As people add more and more 'connections', the web becomes quite complex. Try to cultivate an atmosphere where people are willing to make tentative suggestions as well as safe ones.

When you have done this, discuss some of the connections that came out of the exercise and what you learned from looking at them.

# 26 Fridge magnet psalms

Nearly everyone I know has magnets on their fridges. Gazing at my own rather absent-mindedly one day, I found myself trying to do a fridge magnet 'translation' of a hymn and that started me thinking about their possibilities as a tool to help us understand the psalms better.

## Resources

You will need: some fridge magnets and metal trays to place them on. Alternatively, if you don't find it easy to collect a reasonably large collection of diverse magnets, you could do this same activity using cut-out words and phrases (chop up a photocopy of some psalms or cut out some words from newspapers or magazines) or cut out small pictures.

## Method

You might like to put people into twos or threes to do this activity. Get them a few lines from a psalm they wish to 'interpret'. Allow them some time and space to create their work, 'interpreting' the psalm (or putting it into contemporary language and using everyday illustrations) either with their magnets on trays or pictures or words on trays. One of the beautiful things about using a collection of cut-out words is that when your vocabulary is limited you really have to think carefully about how you are going to say what you really want to say in the words available. This has the by-product of making it impossible just to slip into cliché mode. You have to think about every line carefully.

When the groups are finished with their creations, share them with one another.

## Variation

A variation on this is to 'interpret' well-known hymns or praise songs. Sometimes these can turn into new and wonderful prayers.

# 27  Fruits of the Spirit installations

We did this as a set of teaching installations during a service one Sunday evening. One of the plus points of doing things this way was that people had a chance to read more information than we could easily have given them verbally – not to mention the opportunity to enjoy eating some fruit!

## Resources

You will need: nine pieces of paper printed with the text for each 'station'; nine different types of fruit chopped into small pieces and placed by each 'station'; a dictionary of quotations (which you should be able to borrow from your local library if you don't have one); a thesaurus (you could borrow this from your library too, or use the web).

## Method

Before your service or meeting starts, create the nine 'stations' on pieces of paper. It's a good idea to print these out on A4 sheets and then enlarge them to A3 size so that they are easy to read.

On each sheet write the name of one fruit of the Spirit in large letters: love, joy, peace, patience, kindness, goodness, faithfulness, gentleness and self-control. Then look these up in a dictionary or thesaurus and add some definitions. For example, when you look up 'love' in a thesaurus you will get words like 'adore, cherish, hold dear, treasure, prize, be fond of, care for, like, desire, want, think the world of' and so on. List all you can discover underneath.

Then look for some quotations from different parts of the Bible, from books or films, or perhaps from famous Christians or leaders from your dictionary of quotations. Choose quotes that really amplify the meaning of the word. For example, Julian of Norwich wrote this about love: *What was our Lord's meaning? Learn it well: Love was His meaning. Who showed it you? Love. What did he show you? Love. Why did he show it you? For Love* (paraphrased from *Revelations of Divine Love*).

When you have created your sheets about each fruit, place each of them in a different part of your building or church, so that people can wander around visiting each one in turn. Place a bowl of fruit pieces by each station too, and invite people to take a piece of fruit when they have read the text. It's good to have a different fruit placed by each of these stations; and, where possible, fruit that relates to the text in some way. For example, we used strawberries for love as they are heart shaped and bananas for joy – with a bit of imagination they look like smiling lips!

When all your stations are ready, begin your session by reading Galatians 5:13–25. Then invite everyone to visit any stations, in any order (otherwise traffic-jams will form!).

# 28  Quote cards

The idea behind these cards is to use them as a method of stimulating discussion on a Bible passage – any Bible passage really, as long as it has characters and action in it. This activity wouldn't be so good for looking at the Psalms, for example.

Because using the cards involves an element of chance, there is plenty of opportunity for results to be amusing or poignant, or for your conversation to take directions you might never have explored.

### Resources

You will need: Bibles (one per person, preferably); a set of cards with the quotes (page 70) on them (one per card). Once you've tried this out once you might like to change or remove some of these quotes, and add more quotes of your own.

You can make your cards by photocopying the quotes (enlarged if possible) onto card, or you can write them on stickers on a cheap pack of playing cards.

### Method

Choose a Bible passage to discuss; then shuffle the quote cards and get one person in the group to pick one from the pack. Suppose he chooses *I'm terrified.* Ask the group whether they can picture any character in that Bible passage saying or thinking *I'm terrified.* If so, which character and why?

With some passages, the answers may be obvious. For example, if you are working on the passage about Jesus appearing to the disciples after the resurrection and you choose *I don't believe it!* then it will be easy to put those words into the mouth of Thomas. But at other times you may have to think a little harder. Sometimes the quote you have picked will not fit your passage at all. That's absolutely OK – just pick another card!

When you have exhausted the discussion for one quote, simply pick another quote to discuss and see if that gives you insights into other aspects of the passage. At the end of your discussion you may like to make a list of all the quotes you wished *had* been there in that passage. You may decide to add some of these quotes to your cards for another occasion.

# 29  Treasuring the questions

(with thanks to Sharon Stinson and the Community of Action and Contemplation in New Mexico)

We first used this activity at a service when Sharon was a guest speaker. As a member of the congregation, I was a little nervous about what was going to happen at first, feeling wary that some people might ask rude or irreverent questions. But actually I was amazed at the profound and wonderful questions that people posed for us – many of which seemed to begin with the words, 'I wonder… ' followed by something I had never noticed about a gospel story I had read many times.

### Resources

You will need: no special resources, but having the Bible reading in front of everyone, perhaps using an OHP, is very helpful, as will be a roving or cordless microphone if you are meeting in a larger building.

### Method

Appoint a good reader to read the Bible passage. For this activity a reading from one of the Gospels is particularly good, but it could be from another part of the Bible. A good example is Mark 6:30–34, 53–56.

After the reading, encourage everyone to adopt a prayerful posture. Relax and pray a preparation prayer asking God to come and speak to everyone. A simple song may be appropriate at this point, or a short repeated prayer such as, 'Come, Lord Jesus'.

After this, invite anyone who would like to, to pose a question about the passage. Everyone else should be quiet, listen to the questions, ponder them, but not answer them in any way. It is important for people to feel that their questions are not being belittled, but being valued as genuine. Questions should be short; this is not an opportunity for making statements or giving sermons. Space needs to be left between each question for silent prayer.

It may be appropriate to answer some questions at a later time, or to discuss them. Some questions may not have answers. But that does not matter. We will find out the answers one day, possibly not this side of heaven. The point of this activity is to raise questions which make people think and pray through the passage more deeply.

# 30 Abstract art Bible pictures

This is another way of interpreting Scripture visually, hopefully turning it into prayer and discussion as well. The great thing about abstract art and, ironically, often the thing that people complain about when they visit galleries, is that anyone can do it! You don't have to be able to draw, just express yourself through colour and line. And that can be a valuable aid to expressing ourselves in prayer and worship.

### Resources
You will need: paper; paint (children's poster paints are fine); brushes; newspaper to put around to prevent too much mess; postcards from art galleries or any books with abstract pictures in them (these could be borrowed from the library); Bibles.

### Method
Choose some Bible passages that are full of emotional intensity. In theory, you could choose any part of the Bible, but if you choose a historical part of the Bible, or an incident from the Gospels, people may be tempted not to express it in an abstract way.

Any of the psalms are particularly good to try this with, but especially Psalms 9, 22, 33, 130 and 150. Lamentations or the prophets both have some very poignant passages within them. Song of Songs has some wonderful, worshipful passages full of love, or you may wish to try expressing the hope within Romans 8 in abstract art.

When you have chosen some passages, show your group examples of the work of some abstract artists. (You may like to look in particular at Kandinsky, Jackson Pollock and Mondrian.) Pass around the books or postcards. Remind people that it is the quality of their prayer and worship that is important, not the quality of their painting or drawing.

Ask people to think about the mood of the chosen Bible passages. This helps people to not be too literal. As they paint, you might like to play some gentle music to help people to relax into what is probably quite a new activity for them.

When everyone has finished their paintings, give an opportunity for anyone to share their work, but do not force anyone either to paint or to share. Some people might simply like to watch others. You may find that sharing those artistic interpretations of passages might lead to some very interesting discussions in itself. So make sure you leave time for this.

## Variation

A variation on this idea, particularly for those who are feeling a little shy about painting, is to get a collection of art postcards or books of abstract art and choose examples painted by other artists to complement a Bible passage of their choice. This leaves less of a chance for prayer and worship through doing the painting, but can lead to some interesting conversations.

# 31 Sound and psalms

This is a way of using music and psalms to stimulate worship and discussion. The Psalms are an amazing collection of hymns to God, encompassing huge breadth and depth of emotions within them. Sometimes it's difficult for us to appreciate this when we just say them or sing them in only one sort of way. Playing different sorts of music behind them can make us better appreciate their emotional impact.

## Resources

You will need: a CD player or stereo system; two music CDs (or you could use live musicians); Bibles (one per person, preferably); a collection of simple instruments such as guitar, maracas, rain stick, tambourine, chime bars, shakers or any other percussion instruments (optional).

## Method

Choose a psalm and two pieces of music expressing different emotions. Psalm 2, for example, can be read angrily or sadly. Try reading it once with a poignant piece of music behind it, such as Barber's *Adagio for Strings*, then with something more strident such as 'Mars' from the *Planet Suite* by Holst.

Read the text of the psalm slowly, allowing a short pause after the end of each phrase for the meaning to sink in. When you have finished, discuss the difference in listening to these two versions. What did you notice about the psalm from the different ways it was read?

You don't need to confine yourself to any one psalm; try a few of them. Nor do you need to restrict yourself to classical music. You can use rock music, blues, pop or dance music. Music with lyrics generally doesn't work as it is too off-putting having to compete with sung lyrics. An exception to this rule can be made if the lyrics are in a different language such as Latin.

If you are feeling adventurous, you could try as a group to compose some simple music to put behind a psalm to bring out the meaning you have found within it. You don't have to be great musicians to do this; it can be done simply with percussion. It doesn't have to be tuneful, it can be quite avant-garde if you wish. Just add sound textures that lend menace or mystery or joy to the reading of the psalm. Don't think that you have to compose a tune to fit the words of the psalm; it is much easier to let someone simply read the words to the accompaniment of your musical backing. As with the use of clay or paint, it is the quality of your prayer that is important – not the perfection of your musical ability.

# 32 Walking the Bible

This idea came about thanks to having to walk my dog every day! Walking around our local country park, I sometimes found myself quite naturally falling into some kind of rhythm in my prayers. Sometimes it's hard to know what to pray in a given situation and so I would simply pray, 'Lord-have-mer-cy, Christ-have-mer-cy', as I walked.

This technique can also be used with the Bible. Any verse that is fairly short and has a good rhythm can be walked with.

## Resources

You will need: nothing special apart from a Bible and somewhere to walk – hopefully somewhere pleasant! Also (optional) paper and pencil.

**Method**

Choose some short Bible verses that you want to meditate on or get to know better. This could be a phrase or two from a passage you've read recently; or perhaps some words of Jesus in the Gospels; or part of a psalm. They need to be verses that work with the two-beat rhythm of your walking. You may want to write them down on a piece of paper to take with you.

As you walk, become aware of the steady rhythm of your footsteps: 1-2, 1-2. Then place your words into that rhythm.

Here's an example:

| | |
|---|---|
| left foot | I |
| right foot | am |
| left foot | the |
| right foot | bread |
| left foot | of |
| right foot | life |

John 6:48

Or:

| | |
|---|---|
| left foot | I |
| right foot | am |
| left foot | the |
| right foot | way |
| left foot | and |
| right foot | the |
| left foot | truth |
| right foot | and |
| left foot | the |
| right foot | life |

John 14:6

It doesn't matter if your phrase has an uneven number of syllables; you just have to begin on a different foot on the repetition. A great by-product of doing this activity is that you will probably have memorised the verse by the end of walking with it for a while. More importantly, you will have had a chance to pray about it and ponder its meaning in relation to your life.

# 33  Psalm calligraphy

A friend of mine enjoys calligraphy and this gave me the idea for this creative way of interpreting psalms. As with many of these prayer and worship ideas, remember that you don't have to be particularly artistic to have a go: it is the quality of your thoughts and prayers that are important, not the quality of your artwork.

**Resources**

You will need: Bibles for everyone; paper. You might decide to have nice textured watercolour paper for this or coloured paper, or black paper that you can write in on gold. Also: rough paper (to try ideas out on) is also useful; pens. These could be ink pens, but could you just as easily use fibre-tipped or rollerball pens. Ballpoints probably wouldn't suit. Also: gold and silver or pearlised gel pens are fun to use. Optional: some appropriate instrumental music to play.

**Method**

Ask each person in your group to choose a section of a psalm that they find meaningful. Explain that there are many creative ways of presenting words. Medieval monks spent ages making their manuscripts look attractive, a major feature being to make the first letter of each page or chapter into a picture. The Celts used to decorate the borders of their pages with knotwork and fantastical animals. Muslim calligraphers, forbidden by their religious beliefs to make any pictorial representations at all, used to make the writing itself large and elaborate, like a huge pattern.

These days, calligraphers have lots of freedom. For example, they can make the writing curve into the shape of whatever they are writing about – be that a mountain, a rose, a stream or just a geometric shape like a spiral or zigzag. They can change ink colour whenever they like; they can write in lots of different shapes, sizes and styles on the same page.

Different moods can be reflected in writing style. Angry psalms can be written in spiky letters. Verses about the creation of the natural world can be made small, detailed and delicate.

Having introduced the subject, it would be really helpful to show some examples of different calligraphy styles. Downloads from the Internet or books from your local library will provide sources for illuminated manuscripts and different scripts.

Give out both the rough and the good paper and encourage everyone to plan and experiment with their rough paper first, before they do their 'best' version. Then simply give them time and space to create their psalm calligraphy.

When everyone has done a page, some may wish to share what they have done and tell the others why they interpreted their psalm in the way they did. This may lead to some interesting discussions, particularly as other people may pick up themes unnoticed by others. Be careful not to criticise or belittle anyone's artwork as you share, but be positive and encouraging to everyone.

# 34 Washing our dreams

We did this prayer idea in a church service which was about our plans for the future. When all the pieces of material had been hung up on the washing line it made a wonderful art installation across the church building!

### Resources
You will need: some pieces of light coloured scrap material; clothes pegs; a washing line (strong string is fine); a bowl of water; some pens that will write on fabric without the writing washing out – either fabric pens or ballpoint pens.

### Method
Get a good reader to read **The dream washing script** (page 49).

# 35 Padlock

### Resources
You will need: a small length of metal chain (a thick chain works best); a padlock with a key. You may need a number of these, as sometimes people can take a while 'sharing' and queues can build up. Also: paper and pencils or pens; bins.

### Method
Read Matthew 16:13–19, then get a good reader to read **The padlock script** (page 50).

# 36  Bark

Tree bark is a poignant symbol of dryness, yet it often has such beautiful patterns and textures. We have found it to be a great reminder about our need of God and what happens when we try to live life without him.

### Resources
You will need: some pieces of old bark; a cross; some plants, greenery or small trees in tubs for decoration; a bowl of small pieces of fruit (grapes are ideal).

### Method
Place the cross at the front of your meeting space so that everyone can see it. Surround it with greenery. Invite everyone to pass the bark around so that people can look at and touch it during the meditation. Then get two readers to read **The bark script** (page 51).

# 37  Rolling out the red carpet

This is a good way of praying and preparing for Christmas, a way of trying to find out what 'preparing the way of the Lord' might mean for us in our time and our culture.

### Resources
You will need: a few metres of red material (lining material is good for this); if you want to make your 'carpet' longer, then split the material lengthways to make a longer strip. Also: dark coloured felt-tips; newspaper. Be aware that the felt-tips will bleed slightly on the fabric.

### Method
Decide where to put your red carpet. If your church building has an aisle, then this is an ideal place. Place newspaper on the ground to prevent the ink soaking through and damaging the floor or carpet. Then roll out your red material.

Appoint a good reader to read Isaiah 40:1–5. Then ask another reader to read **The red carpet script** (page 52), pausing at the end of each paragraph.

# 38  House plan

### Resources
You will need: a plan of a typical house. If you know an architect you could ask him to donate a professional one. Alternatively, you could either draw your own simple plan or photocopy the one provided (page 55). Also: coloured stickers or people shapes with Blu-Tack. When I first thought of this prayer activity, I planned to have people put their initials on the house plan, but a member of the group suggested using coloured stickers instead, which was actually much more meaningful and gave people some privacy if they wished to remain anonymous. As an alternative, on the plan we've provided little person outlines that you may want to photocopy and use.

### Method
Explain that this will be a time of offering yourselves and your friends to God by placing symbols on a house plan. The plan is used as a prayer aid to pray for each person in the group. Appoint a good reader to read **The house plan script** (page 54). You may like to look up and discuss some of the Bible passages mentioned, or add others of your own choosing.

# 39 The Lord's Prayer with props

This idea works best in a small group situation. It's a way of discovering new meaning in this wonderful prayer using ordinary household items as props to help our thought processes.

You can use any props you like, and you'll see examples of some of the props I have used below. In fact, you may find that discussing what props to use before you pray is the most interesting part of the whole exercise!

If using this prayer activity with a large congregation, you could put pictures of some of these items up on the flip chart, OHP or video projector as you pray, rather than using the real props, making sure you give space for reflection on each image. If each line of the prayer was printed alongside the image, people would know when to say the next line.

## Resources

You will need: props for each line of the prayer; the text of the prayer either visible at the front or given out as photocopies (it's harder to say by heart when you pause between lines).

Suggestions:

| | |
|---|---|
| Our Father in heaven, | a picture of a parent and child |
| hallowed be your name, | an honours board, prize-giving programme, or picture of Oscar or Nobel peace prize being presented |
| your kingdom come, | a national flag or a postage stamp |
| your will be done | a recent newspaper, a dog lead or a map |
| on earth as it is in heaven. | picture of earth from space or a newspaper |
| Give us today our daily bread. | a loaf or pictures of food, clothing and houses |
| Forgive us our debts, | a toy gun or toy handcuffs |
| as we also have forgiven our debtors, | a cross |
| And lead us not into temptation, | adverts for expensive things |
| but deliver us from evil. | a bottle labelled 'poison' (note: don't use a real poison bottle!) |
| For yours is the kingdom | a crown (which could be paper) |
| and the power | foreign money, a toy weapon or picture of Parliament |
| and the glory | a palm branch or picture of fans at a concert or football match |
| for ever. Amen. | a stopped clock |

## Method

When you have discussed what props you are going to use, gather them together, placing them in the centre of your group. As you pray each line of the prayer, pass the appropriate item around your group, pausing long enough for it to make its journey around everyone, finally returning the items to the middle of the room. Use the time to reflect on the items, and the meaning of that line of the prayer.

# 40 Anchor of hope

This is a practical prayer activity about holding onto hope through the tough times. It works best in a large group or church service.

### Resources

You will need a strong thick rope (like a towrope) long enough for everyone to hold onto; something to attach the rope to that can hold it firmly (a strong bracket, hook or pillar); an anchor (this doesn't have to be real, but could be cut out of cardboard and painted black).

### Method

Attach your rope and your anchor to the bracket, hook or pillar. If you can make it look as if the anchor is holding the rope, then so much the better; otherwise just hang it from the rope so that it can be seen. Trail the rope across your building.

Read Hebrews 6:13–20 and explain that the activity that follows will be symbolic. You could say that Abraham held onto the hope of having many descendants throughout all the years that he was childless. For us, our ultimate hope is the hope of heaven – the hope of being with God for ever. This hope can sometimes keep us going when things are tough.

Invite everyone to hold onto that hope of heaven symbolically, by holding onto the anchor line stretched along the church. Be aware of the safety issues. Ask the congregation or group not to pull on the line too hard, as the fixing may come out, or someone might fall!

You may then wish to use the simple piece of liturgy below, or your own prayer with a very easy response that does not need printed words.

### The Anchor of Hope Prayer

When life is hard and we can't see the future

**we hold on to the anchor of hope in you.**

When everyone around us laughs at our beliefs

**we hold on to the anchor of hope in you.**

When everything we touch seems to end in disaster

**we hold on to the anchor of hope in you.**

When we're suffering illness or tiredness or stress

**we hold on to the anchor of hope in you.**

When tears fill our lives and our hearts are grieving

**we hold on to the anchor of hope in you.**

When we're feeling lonely or far from our friends

**we hold on to the anchor of hope in you.**

When times are good and we start being forgetful

**we hold on to the anchor of hope in you.**   Amen.

# 41  The calming of the storm

This is an imaginative Bible meditation based on the calming of the storm narrative in Mark 4. It aims to recreate the experience of one of the disciples travelling with Jesus, calling up the sounds, sights, smells and experiences he may have encountered as he went on that eventful journey.

### Resources

You will need: no special resources apart from the script and a Bible.

### Method

Begin by ensuring everyone is comfortable and relaxed and then read Mark 4:35–41 to set the scene for **The storm script** (page 53).

# 42 Sour grapes

This meditation is based on Isaiah 5:1–7 and is an example of how you can take a Bible parable and turn it into a modern scenario giving fresh emotional impact on people who may be very familiar with the reading. The purpose here is to inspire intercession for our broken world. You can choose to read the original passage before the meditation, but reading it afterwards will perhaps give added intrigue. You can use the same technique with any of Jesus' parables.

### Resources

You will need: no special resources apart from a good reader, **The sour grapes script** (page 56) and a Bible.

# 43 Fire and water

This is a multi-sensory meditation on the Holy Spirit. We first used these oil lamps at a service for Pentecost and were amazed at how the flames seemingly float on the water.

### Resources

You will need: plastic wick holders and wicks for water and oil lamps. These are available cheaply as little kits from good candle shops or craft shops; be sure to follow carefully the safety instructions on the packet. Also: clear glass bowls; a jug of water; olive oil; some gentle instrumental music to play in the background; the script.

### Method

Pour some water from the jug dramatically into the clear bowl while saying **The fire and water script** (page 57) based on John 4:13,14 and John 7:37–39.

# 44 Multi-Sensory Gospels

One method of praying with the Bible is to use your imagination to bring a Gospel story to life. This makes us notice things about the events recorded in the Gospels that we have not noticed before, and it also draws us into the action with a more emotional response, instead of merely spectating or switching off because we know a passage so well. This method of imagining yourself as a character in a Bible story was pioneered by Ignatius in the sixteenth century, and the particular variation I am using here uses each of the five senses in turn to look at a passage.

### Resources

You will need: no special resources apart from Bibles and one or more good readers, preferably allowed some time to look at the script in advance.

### Method

Choose a story from the Gospels and read it a couple of times either silently or out loud to get the feel of the passage. Then get yourself into a comfortable position where you can begin to imagine the story and bring it to life. Remember: you are not interested in creating a perfect historical reproduction; you are interested in meeting Jesus and learning more about him through the Bible. When you are comfortable, pray that Jesus will show you new things through the passage. Then begin to use your imagination. As an example, I am going to use the account of the raising of Lazarus from death in John 11:17–44.

Read **The Lazarus script** (page 58) fairly slowly so that everyone has time to imagine these events properly. Tell everyone they are bystanders in positions where they can see everything. The script starts with focusing on the sense of sight – imagining what might have been seen by someone actually there.

# 45 Perspectives

Using your imagination to become involved with a character in the Bible can really change your perspective. By moving from focusing on one person in the account to another, you gain valuable insights.

This example takes two people's different perspectives and is a creative and fresh way of taking a group of people through a Bible passage; here it's the well-known story of the healing of the paralysed man.

## Resources
You will need: no special resources apart from Bibles and a good reader.

## Method
Explain to people that this is not about totally accurate historical re-enactment. It's about us learning more about Jesus, getting close to the action so that we can notice the things he's teaching.

Begin by reading Mark 2:1–12 out loud, with everyone else either listening or following in Bibles. Then read **The man on the stretcher script** (page 60) slowly and with frequent pauses, especially at the questions, to allow people time to recreate the situation in their minds.

# 46 Clay

We love using clay as a prayer tool as it is so wonderfully tactile – although you do have be prepared for a bit of mess! Using clay does seem to have a wide appeal across all age ranges.

## Resources
You will need: a lump of clay for each person. You could use 'new' clay which contains nylon fibres and is a little less messy than ordinary clay, or modelling clay, but real clay is best. Also: some boards on which to work the clay (large plates or trays would do); small bowls of water in which people can wet their fingers; washing facilities. Additionally, you may like to have a digital camera at hand to record some of the results, but remember to ask permission first.

## Method
Read Jeremiah 18:1–6.

Give everyone who wants to take part a piece of clay, and ask them to mould a shape that represents something they want to change about themselves inside. (Note: *not* something physical about themselves!) The shape could represent a bad habit they want to get rid of, or a good intention that never seems to come to fruition. Remind the group that this is a prayer activity, and so the quality or cleverness of the sculpture is not important. Suggest that they shouldn't try to be too literal with the clay. As an example, someone might decide to mould a spiky shape which is symbolic of their struggle with anger.

It is useful to warn people fairly soon in the process that their creations are going to be changed as the session goes on, so they don't get too possessive about their work!

When everyone has had sufficient time to create something, ask the group to spend a few minutes thinking about the fact that God loves them beyond measure; that he cares for them – even with all those difficult or bad habits inside. He loves them just as they are.

Then ask the group to swap their piece of clay with someone else. Get them to wet their fingers a little, and smooth the clay shape they now have gently and lovingly. As they do, ask them to pray for the person who created the shape, that God would heal and help them with whatever struggles they are having.

Finally, ask the group to swap a second time and then, using this different clay piece, make a shape that is symbolic of the sort of person they think God wants them to be – a new creation. This doesn't have to be a human figure. It could be a flower, tree, fruit or just an abstract symbol.

As they are doing this, ask each person to pray for all the others in the group, asking God that he would use them to mould and help the others grow and become more Christlike – perfect, loving and holy.

# 47 Feathers

This was inspired by some words from the remarkable Abbess Hildegard of Bingen (1098–1179). She once said that she was 'a feather on the breath of God' and that started me thinking about what a powerful image feathers are.

## Resources

You will need: a collection of feathers. Any feathers will do but small ones work best; coloured feathers are available from art or craft shops. Also: two good readers.

## Method

Give a feather to each person. Then ask your two readers to read **The feathers script** (page 62) – Reader 1 reading the meditation pieces, Reader 2 the Bible verses.

# 48 Holy Week smell trail

Smell is an amazing sense. Just a faint wisp of a smell that you have not encountered for years can stimulate your memory in an amazing way, perhaps taking you back to your childhood. This smell trail is designed to do that for us in a spiritual way, taking us back to the most important week in history.

## Resources

You will need: nine cassette tapes and players; fireguards (as a safety measure for some exhibits); a bottle of fairly strong and exotic-smelling perfume and a dish to pour it into; some frankincense burning in a censer or frankincense oil in a pot of hot water; ashes from the remains of a fire (still warm if possible! – make sure you are keeping them safely in a metal container); a bowl of very soapy water; some bitter herbs (sprigs of fresh rosemary and/or thyme oil in a pot of hot water); fresh baked (preferably unleavened) bread (soda bread is fine); a small jug of wine; olives; a jar of wine vinegar; some myrrh oil (add aloe vera, too, if you wish) in a pot of hot water; a pan of freshly fried fish; a slice of roast lamb (optional); a little olive oil in a pot of hot water (optional).

## Method

There is quite a bit of advance preparation to do for this activity. You need to bake (or buy freshly baked) bread. You will also need to fry some fish. We used a portable stove to do this, so that it was nice and fresh, but remember that you will need to light a fire and allow time for it to cool again; be extremely careful with fire safety. Probably the best thing to do is to get some paper and wooden kindling, light it in a barbecue and then allow it to cool until it is safe. You will also need to set up pots of hot water for the scented oils. We usually use boiling water from the kettle which spreads the scent nicely without the need to have candles or oil burners. When you set up some of the smells, for example the freshly fried fish and the fire ashes, it would be wise to set up some sort of fireguard, just to make sure that no one accidentally touches anything hot, or knocks over any hot water.

The best way to arrange this trail is as a set of installations around the church building. You can print the meditations (page 63) on pieces of paper, but this does mean that you have to have your eyes open while you are reading them. It's more effective if you can record the meditations onto cassette tapes and play them, either on a small portable stereos with the volume kept fairly low or, with smaller groups of people, you can play the meditations on personal stereos.

You need to think quite carefully about where you are going to place the installations for the smell trail. They need to be far enough away from each other for the smells and the sound of the tapes not to disturb each other. You may find it useful to post a map by the entrance of your building or room, so that people can find the various installations.

# 49  The Exodus journey

I got the idea for this method of praying with scripture when I was on holiday in France a few years ago. In Lyons there was a 'rosary garden'. A pathway snaking down the hill was planted with brass roses set into the ground at regular intervals along the route. People were encouraged to use the garden like a set of rosary beads, thinking and praying about different incidents from the lives of Jesus and Mary as they walked to different parts of the garden. I was sure that something along those lines could be adapted for any long pathway, walk or journey.

## Resources

You will need: a pathway or route (this could be in a garden, a country path, along a beach or in the grounds of your accommodation during a church houseparty weekend); signs with meditations written on them, perhaps decorated with pictures or marked with props or sculptures (you could put these in plastic sleeves to protect them from the weather and weigh them down with stones). If you are unable to get permission to set up temporary signs you could photocopy a booklet with the meditations in and use existing landmarks as your markers, such as 'Move on to meditation 2 when you reach the old bridge'.

## Method

Walk your path in advance, marking points at regular intervals as good places to stop and pray. Then write meditations for each of the stopping points. There's no need for these to be too long – people will be able to fill in any gaps using their own imaginations.

It might be a good idea to check the weather forecast in advance before planning your journey, and make sure people are prepared for the weather not to be perfect!

Arrange for everyone to meet up at a certain place and time to begin the walk, but you will probably find that everyone's journey is more prayerful if start times are staggered.

Allow plenty of time for the slower walkers in your group to find their way along the pathway. Locate a suitable place at the end of the journey where people can congregate and perhaps have some refreshments. Encourage people to share anything they have learned from going on the journey and anything God has shown them through it.

I have included some sample meditations for a 10-station journey based on the Exodus (page 71), which could be adapted if you have a shorter path. And activity 50 gives a 10-station journey based on the life of Elijah. But I encourage you to try creating your own. Some other suggestions for subjects around which you could create meditative journeys:

- Jesus' journey to Jerusalem

- Paul's travels as recorded in Acts

- the life of Christ

- Christ's entry into Jerusalem, his betrayal, death and resurrection

# 50  The Elijah journey

This is another Bible journey (page 74) that you can take by journeying around a large garden, a country path or a beach. For details of resources and method, see activity 49.

# The scarlet and snow script

This is a creative confession prayer; an opportunity for us to be able to say sorry to God for anything that we are personally feeling guilty about, or a chance to apologise for the actions of our society and the part that we sometimes play in society's wrongdoings.

If you'd like to get into a comfortable position, I'll begin by reading a passage from the book of Isaiah. At the end I'll read another extract from the same book.

> *Your hands are full of blood;*
> > *wash and make yourselves clean.*
> *Take your evil deeds*
> > *out of my sight!*
> *Stop doing wrong,*
> > *learn to do right!*
> *Seek justice,*
> > *encourage the oppressed.*
> *Defend the cause of the fatherless,*
> > *plead the case of the widow.*
>
> Isaiah 1:15b–17

Now I'd like to invite you to contemplate the red paper for a few minutes and think of some things you'd like to confess to God. Use the pencils to write anything you like on the paper. You can describe the sin in a few words if you are feeling brave, or use the initials of the sin, or simply write symbols that only mean something between you and God. If you prefer, you can write a description of one of society's corporate sins. Or you can just watch and pray quietly. It's up to you.

Pause for a while to give everyone a chance to write anything they wish on the paper. Then ask for a volunteer to sprinkle some talc over the writing, blotting it out, while you read the next part of the Bible passage.

> *'Come now, let us reason together,'*
> > *says the LORD.*
> *'Though your sins are like scarlet,*
> > *they shall be as white as snow;*
> *though they are red as crimson,*
> > *they shall be like wool.*
> *If you are willing and obedient,*
> > *you will eat the best from the land … '*
>
> Isaiah 1:18,19

(Pause for contemplation)

The great thing about this confession prayer is that you don't just get to *see* the paper and the talc. You also get the wonderful *smell* of the talc, which is especially poignant if you use baby talc. The whole room is filled with a subtle fragrance which is a reminder of childhood innocence and bath time – which in itself might make us think of baptism and sins being washed away.

# The confession script

Get into a comfortable position where you are able to think and pray easily. Now imagine that you are in first-century Palestine. You sense the warm air. The sounds of traffic (or other local noises, mentioned as appropriate) disappear and are replaced by the bustle of a first-century town. You find yourself in front of Jesus, dragged to him by a large, noisy crowd of people. They hold you before him. You can't move to run away from him. You are scared. Kneeling before God, you can't lie; you are faced with your deepest, darkest secrets, and the fact that he knows them too. All the rubbish you have ever done in your life… everything you have ever done or said… he knows about. He knows all about…

– the sweets you took from the newsagent…

– that kid you bullied at school…

– the times you talked unkindly behind your friend's back…

– the way you hurt your family…

He knows about them all…

– the things that shame you more than you can say…

– the wrong things you have thought… and said… and done. . .

He can see your heart…

Take a moment to remember the things you have done wrong, recently or in the past, and make a written or drawn symbol to represent them in the tray of sand in front of you. (Pause for activity)

A voice behind you shouts out your sins to God and the rest of the crowd. You cower away from him, ashamed to be kneeling before perfection. You look at the ground, afraid to meet God's eyes as he looks at you. But he reaches out to you and raises your head, so you have no choice but to look at him. His eyes never leave yours as he reaches down to brush over the sand where you wrote your confession.

Gently shake the tray of sand.

The sand is unmarked. Your sins have disappeared for ever. No one else can ever know what you had written there.

God turns to face the crowd.

'Are any of you perfect? Has anyone here never sinned? Do you have the right to judge any one of my people? Leave judgement to God in heaven. Try to live out the faith you have, rather than condemn other people.'

The people turn to leave, and you are released. God kneels next to you; he looks at you. Beyond your sins he sees your laughter, your smile, your tears… your heart. He sees beauty hidden where you could only see your sins. Tears fall from his eyes as he sees your pain. Silently he wraps his arms around you, holds you tightly and leads you to a safe place.

Before you leave, you may wish light a candle to symbolise your acceptance of the forgiveness offered to you.

# The mirror script

Jesus said, *The eye is the lamp of the body. If your eyes are good, your whole body will be full of light. But if your eyes are bad, your whole body will be full of darkness.* (Matthew 6:22)

This candle symbolises the light of Christ and the mirror symbolises ourselves and our lives. As we come to worship, many of us might be finding it hard to see the light of Jesus' love at the moment. Maybe we're feeling that our eyesight is poor. Things might be getting in the way… worries… thoughts about the million and one things that we have to do today… doubts… fears… things we have done wrong that we are feeling guilty about…

In your own time, write or draw onto the mirror any of those things that are on your mind, or just colour in a segment of mirror if you don't wish to write or draw. This is an opportunity for us to talk to God about those things that are getting in the way of us seeing him clearly.

Pause to allow people to come and add whatever they wish. You may like to play a piece of music or a song about repentance during this time.

Jesus said, *You are the light of the world. A city on a hill cannot be hidden. Neither do people light a lamp and put it under a bowl. Instead they put it on its stand, and it gives light to everyone in the house. In the same way, let your light shine before others, that they may see your good deeds and praise your Father in Heaven.* (Matthew 5:14–16, slightly changed to make it inclusive)

I am now going to clean off the glass. As I do so, let's silently pray that God takes away all the things that are getting in the way of us seeing God's light and reflecting it so that other people may see God working in us. Amen.

# The thistles script

The Parable of the Sower often concentrates us on our own faith; how to spread it; and how to be fruitful. But in this meditation we are going to think about something else: the seed that was choked by the weeds.

In the first parable, the Parable of the Sower, Jesus uses thorns to symbolise worries and wealth. In the second parable, the Parable of the Weeds – also about seed – Jesus uses thorns to symbolise wickedness.

Let's spend a few minutes thinking about the seeds we sow. Are they always good seeds? In Galatians 6:7, Paul says we will reap what we sow. Think about all the times you may have sown bad seed: angry words, gossip, worrying rumours, mistrust, or anything else that comes to mind.

(Pause)

Now take a minute to remember the Parable of the Sower once more. Think of the devastating effects that  bad seeds can have, choking the plants.

(Pause)

Jesus said *Do people pick grapes from thornbushes, or figs from thistles? Likewise every good tree bears good fruit, but a bad tree bears bad fruit.* (Matthew 7:16,17).

Place the thistle seed you have been given in the palm of your hand and look at it now. Think about something it could symbolise; perhaps some seeds you wish you hadn't planted. Then, as a sign that we are sorry for times when we have spread seeds of hate rather than love, let's go outside and put those seeds on the fire. As we do so, we will ask God to help us spread the good seed of his gospel instead.

Go outside, inviting everyone to burn their seeds. As you return to the building, you may wish to give out good seed such as sunflowers, nuts or conkers in return for the bad seeds.

# The scripture news script

**Reader 1**    Jeremiah says, *My people are fools; they do not know me.*

**Reader 2**    It was a terrorist action of almost unimaginable brutality.

**Reader 3**    Today I witnessed the unimaginable… the World Trade Center collapsing before my eyes.

**Reader 1**    *They are senseless children; they have no understanding.*

**Reader 2**    Security is tight but there is nothing you can do against an airliner. It was a hopeless situation.

**Reader 3**    I looked behind me and a huge cloud of dust and debris was following me. Soon the cloud was upon me and my mouth and eyes filled with dust and dirt.

**Reader 1**    *They are skilled in doing evil; they know not how to do good.*

**Reader 2**    It took me 30 minutes to get out. I was in the military and I can take stress – but now I just can't stop shaking.

**Reader 1**    *I looked at the earth, and it was formless and empty;*

**Reader 3**    It was like a war zone. There were many injured. Everyone was screaming, crying, running… cops, people, firefighters, everyone…

**Reader 1**    *and (I looked) at the heavens and their light was gone.*

**Reader 2**    The building suddenly collapsed. I just got blown somewhere and then it was total darkness. We tried to get away, but I was blown to the ground. And I was trying to help this woman, but I couldn't find her in the darkness.

**Reader 1**    *I looked at the mountains, and they were quaking; all the hills were swaying. I looked, and there were no people …*

**Reader 2**    Hundreds of police officers and firefighters helping to evacuate those trapped inside lost their lives as the towers collapsed. The mayor said that the death toll would be 'more than any of us can bear'.

**Reader 3**    Survivors walked around like ghosts, covered in dirt, weeping and wandering, dazed.

**Reader 1**    *… every bird in the sky had flown away. I looked, and the fruitful land was a desert; all its towns lay in ruins before the Lord …*

# The plumb line script

*So this is what the Sovereign LORD says:*
*'See, I lay a stone in Zion,*
            *a tested stone,*
*a precious cornerstone for a sure foundation;*
                *the one who trusts will never be dismayed.*
*I will make justice the measuring line*
            *And righteousness the plumb line… '*

Isaiah 28:16,17a

This was a prophecy about Jesus; a prophecy that he would be our foundation stone and that we could trust in him; a prophecy that he would test us about justice and right living and see how we measured up to his standards.

So let's bring our world to God in prayer, knowing just how far we have slipped from his standards in so many ways.

Next, encourage everyone to look at some of the newspapers and magazines you have scattered around, asking them to carefully tear or cut out headlines or articles relating to situations of injustice.

Let's bring our news cuttings to the plumb line and peg them on, as a sign that we want God to straighten out these situations.

Give people a chance to look through all their articles and then peg one or more onto the plumb line. On a practical note, encourage tall people to peg their articles further up, so that smaller people can peg theirs further down! You could finish with a song or with a Bible passage about God sorting out injustice, such as Isaiah 42:1–4.

## Variation
Alternatively, you may want to give people a chance to write their own prayers about situations of injustice in the world and peg them onto the line.

# The scrapping injustice script

*Why do the nations conspire*
*and the peoples plot in vain?*
*The kings of the earth take their stand*
*and the rulers gather together against the LORD*
*and against his Anointed One.*

Psalm 2:1,2

Next read out some current examples of national leaders who treat their people cruelly.

*When he opened the fifth seal, I saw under the altar the souls of those who had been slain because of the word of God and the testimony they had maintained. They called out in a loud voice, 'How long, Sovereign Lord, holy and true, until you judge the inhabitants of the earth and avenge our blood?'*

Revelation 6:9,10

Insert here some recent examples of people who have been killed for their faith in Christ.

*How long will the wicked, O LORD,*
*how long will the wicked be jubilant?*
*They pour out arrogant words;*
*all the evildoers are full of boasting.*
*They crush your people, O LORD;*
*they oppress your inheritance.*

Psalm 94:3–5

Insert current examples of people suffering from oppression.

*They slay the widow and the alien;*
*they murder the fatherless.*
*They say, 'The LORD does not see;*
*the God of Jacob pays no heed.'*

Psalm 94:6,7

Here read out information about people who have been murdered for their faith in different parts of the world.

*Women have been ravished in Zion,*
*and virgins in the towns of Judah.*
*Princes have been hung up by their hands;*
*elders are shown no respect.*

Lamentations 5:11,12

Include here examples of women who have been attacked and pensioners who have been robbed or beaten, either in their own homes or on the streets of our towns and cities.

*Young men toil at the millstones;*
*boys stagger under loads of wood.*
*The elders are gone from the city gate;*
*the young men have stopped their music.*

Lamentations 5:13,14

Cite current examples of children who have to work because of poverty; or places where they have been forced to be child soldiers.

*Rise up, O God, and defend your cause;*
*    remember how fools mock you all day long.*
*Do not ignore the clamour of your adversaries,*
*    the uproar of your enemies, which rises continually.*

Psalm 74:22

Then invite everyone to write on pieces of paper some examples of the evil in the world that they would like God to destroy. Examples might be: famine, war, rape, injustice, torture, landmines, corruption, sex slavery, greed and starvation. Then invite everyone to fling their pieces of paper into the bin – as violently as they like! As they do so they may wish to shout a short proclamation or victory prayer out loud, something like 'Your kingdom come, O God!' or 'Come, Lord Jesus, stamp out injustice!'

Finish the prayer session by reading Revelation 21:1–4 which ends

*He will wipe away every tear from their eyes. There will be no more death or mourning or crying or pain,*
*for the old order of things has passed away.*

# The swords into ploughshares script

This prayer idea is a way for us to pray for situations of conflict around the world. Some of these situations might hit the news regularly. Some situations might be less well known. Here we have a map of the world. I also have a number of news items about various countries to inform our prayers. So let's begin by taking a few minutes to pass these articles around, and inform ourselves about what has been going on in these areas.

(Pause for this to happen)

Now, take a piece of tinfoil and roughly sculpt a weapon out of it. It can be any weapon you like, ancient or modern.

(Wait for weapons to be constructed)

When you have finished sculpting your weapon, place it on the map on a country that you particularly wish to pray for.

(Pause for weapons to be placed)

> *In the last days*
> *the mountain of the LORD's temple will be established*
>          *as chief among the mountains;*
> *it will be raised above the hills,*
>          *and all nations will stream to it.*
>
> *Many peoples will come and say,*
> *'Come let us go up to the mountain of the LORD,*
>          *to the house of the God of Jacob.*
> *He will teach us his ways,*
>          *so that we may walk in his paths.'*
> *The law will go out from Zion,*
>          *the word of the LORD from Jerusalem.*
> *He will judge between the nations*
>          *and will settle disputes for many peoples.*
> *They will beat their swords into ploughshares*
>          *and their spears into pruning hooks.*
> *Nation will not take up sword against nation,*
>          *nor will they train for war any more.*
>
> Isaiah 2:2–4

Now, I want to invite you to come to the front and pick a weapon to re-sculpt into the shape of something useful, like a ploughing tool or a modern tool or kitchen appliance, and place it back on the map. As you do so, pray that God brings peace to these parts of the world soon, just as he has promised that he would.

# The wallet prayers script

First, look at your **bank cards**, if you have them; or your **cash** if you do not have any cards. Pray for the people who work in your bank; that they will have wisdom to invest and lend money wisely; and to always be ethical in everything they do. Then pray for the way **you** use those bank cards. Thank God for all the material things you have been given and pray that you will use your money wisely, to help rather than to hurt others. If you have more than one bank or credit card you may wish to pray for each of them in turn.

Then take out your **shop loyalty cards**. As you look at them, pray for the people who work in those shops, especially people you know. Pray for those who supply goods for the shops, for farmers and factory workers. Pray for the customers.

If you have any **council or library cards**, pray for the people who work for your local council, especially those in positions of power. Pray that they make right decisions about how to spend the money they are given each year. Pray for those working in stressful or difficult areas of the council. Pray for the library staff; that they will be kind and welcoming to people, especially the vulnerable elderly or sick or needy people who visit them. Pray that people who choose books to stock the library will choose good and useful titles.

Look at all the other things in your wallet. The **scribbled notes** with phone numbers on them, the **club membership cards**, the **receipts** for things you have bought recently, the **business cards** you use or have been given. Pray for the people involved in all those areas of your life. Don't be afraid to take some time over doing this.

Finally, if you feel you can, place your wallet or purse on your hands in front of you and raise it up as a sign that you wish to give all these areas of your life to God. Then return it to its usual place, knowing that God is ultimately in charge of all these parts of your life.

# The family tree

# The family tree script

Turn your thoughts towards those people who make up your own family tree – not your literal family, but your *spiritual* family. We are thinking about all those people who have passed the faith on to you.

It may be helpful here for you to present your own completed family tree, based on your own experiences, as an example.

You might want to put Jesus at the top of the tree along with any of the disciples you feel have taught you something significant, just to remind you of the beginnings of the faith.

Who first told you about Jesus? Was it your parents? Was it a friend or a visiting evangelist? Or perhaps you learned about Jesus from reading the Bible, in which case maybe Matthew, Mark, Luke or John might take the credit for being your spiritual parents.

As you write people's names on the tree branches, thank God for them, and pray for those named who are still alive.

Who would your 'aunts and uncles' be? Maybe they are the people who taught you a bit more about your faith, or showed you new things. Write their names on the tree, too. You might include a schoolteacher, or a youth group leader, clergy or more mature Christians who have helped you on your journey of faith. Add in Christian friends who encourage you in the faith or support you in prayer.

Perhaps you might even be able to put 'children' on your tree too, if you have shared your faith with others who have come to know Jesus.

Don't worry if your tree looks a bit chaotic or messy; many people have helped us along the way, and it is good to give them a mention. If you wish, you can colour your tree green as a reminder that, just as Jesus is the vine and we are the branches, the only reason the tree flourishes is that it is connected to him.

When everyone has finished their tree, give them a chance to share it with others. If it is a large group or congregation, split into smaller groups for this part of the exercise.

Finally, you may want to gather all the trees together at the front, so everyone can see the amazing branches we are all connected to in the family of Jesus!

# The Trinity script

This is a chance for us to use our hands to help us to worship and meditate on the Holy Trinity. First, get yourself into a comfortable position, and then place your hand or hands like this. Fold your bottom two fingers down into your palm, then put your three other fingers together to make a triangle shape. Three fingers, one triangle. Three persons, one God.

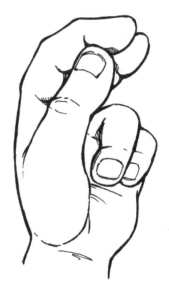

The bottom two fingers folded down onto your palm have a symbolism too. They remind us of what one particular person in the Trinity is like, Jesus Christ. For he has two natures. He is truly God, and truly human too.

Remain with your hands in this position for a while, as we meditate on some scriptures. Although the Trinity is never mentioned by name in the Bible, there are many references to the Father, the Son and the Holy Spirit.

(Pause between each of the Scripture verses)

Jesus said, *I and the Father and I are one* (John 10:30).

*… believe the miracles, that you may know and understand that the Father is in me, and I in the Father* (John 10:38).

*Then God said, 'Let us make man in our image, in our likeness … '* (Genesis 1:26).

*Unless I go away, the Counsellor will not come to you; but if I go, I will send him to you* (John 16:7).

*Now the Lord is the Spirit, and where the Spirit of the Lord is, there is freedom* (2 Corinthians 3:17).

*As Jesus was coming up out of the water, he saw heaven being torn open and the Spirit descending on him like a dove. And a voice came from heaven: 'You are my Son, whom I love … '* (Mark 1:10,11).

*To God's elect … who have been chosen according to the foreknowledge of God the Father, through the sanctifying work of the Spirit, for obedience to Jesus Christ and sprinkling by his blood: Grace and peace be yours in abundance* (1 Peter 1:1,2).

You may wish to finish with a short extract from the Prayer of Saint Patrick (also known as Saint Patrick's Breastplate):

I bind to myself today

The strong virtue of an invocation of the Trinity;

I believe the Trinity in the Unity,

The Creator of the Universe.

Or this simplified version:

I bind unto myself today

The strong name of the Trinity.

By invocation of the same,

The three in one and one in three.

# The dream washing script

I am going to begin this prayer time by reading a passage from the prophet Jeremiah. *'For I know the plans I have for you,'* declares the LORD, *'plans to prosper you and not to harm you, plans to give you hope and a future. Then you will call upon me, and come and pray to me, and I will listen to you. You will seek me and find me when you seek me with all your heart'* (Jeremiah 29:11–13).

We are now going to have a time when we can pray about our own dreams for the future; the prophecies we feel we have been given about our lives; our ambitions for our careers and families in the next few years; the sort of person we would like to become; the places we would like to go; perhaps the dreams we have for using our talents.

As you feel comfortable, take a piece of cloth and draw or write some symbols or words for those dreams on your piece of cloth. Other people may see what you have written, so you may want to write initials or a symbol that has meaning only to you if you feel your dreams are too personal to share.

When you have written about your dreams, come and wash them in the water and, as you do so, ask God to baptise them. Ask him to wash away any dreams or ambitions that may be harmful; ambitions that might ultimately hurt you, other people, or cause you to turn away from God. Then ask God to bless your true dreams, to make something beautiful out of them. Finally, wring out your cloth (so it doesn't drip too much!) and peg it on the washing line as an offering to God.

You may like to light up your washing line in some way, using an overhead projector with a colourful picture on it, or a coloured spotlight.

# The padlock script

In this passage Simon Peter is the first to believe and publicly announce that Jesus is the Christ, and because of that Jesus gives him his new name: Peter the rock. Jesus says that he will build his church on that rock of belief, of faith in Jesus, our foundation stone. He gives Peter and us a new promise: *I will give you the keys of the kingdom of heaven; whatever you bind on earth will be bound in heaven, and whatever you loose on earth will be loosed in heaven* (Matthew 16:19).

Augustine of Hippo had this to say about this passage:

'It wasn't just one man, but rather the One Universal Church that received these keys and the right to "bind" and "loose". If you turn to another place in the Scriptures the same Lord Jesus says to all his apostles, *Receive the Holy Spirit* and afterwards, *If you forgive anyone their sins, they are forgiven; if you do not forgive them, they are not forgiven* (John 20:22,23) or *whatever you bind on earth will be bound in heaven, and whatever you loose on earth will be loosed in heaven* (Matthew 18:18).

'Therefore it is the Church that binds up, the Church that loosens us … Peter was himself three times bound by his fear and cowardice (when he denied Jesus three times before his death) … and Jesus himself loosens him three times by his three questions (*Do you love me?*) and by Peter's answers, in turn, confessing his strong love for Jesus' (paraphrased from Augustine's sermon for the Feast of Peter and Paul).

So now let us think about those things that we really wish we could be loosed from. Perhaps, like Peter, we feel bound by fear; we are afraid of whatever we think God is calling us to do. We can all feel trapped at times. Or maybe you think there is something we as a church are trapped by: bitterness or criticism or any other problem.

Now write some of those things you are feeling trapped by on a piece of paper, being aware that at least one person will see them. You may decide to write initials or symbols of things you do not wish to share with another.

Then team up with a partner, and come to the front of the building where we have a padlock and chain. Place your piece of paper inside the circle made by the locked chain, and then share anything you want to say about the things you have written. Remain silent if you prefer.

Partners, you then pick up the key to the padlock, and say something like 'May Jesus loose you from these chains' while unlocking the padlock. Take the other person's piece of paper from within the chains, scrunch it up and bin it. Then lock the chain and swap roles.

You may want to play some music or sing some songs (perhaps songs about freedom) while this is happening, as it can take some time. Be aware that some people who wish to participate may not be able to find partners so have some people 'primed' ready to offer themselves as partners to those wishing to go to the front.

# The bark script

**Reader 1** Look at your piece of bark, at its texture. Notice the patterns; the areas of light and shadow. Let your fingers feel the ridges and know that this bark was once part of a living tree. Yet now it is dead. If you planted it, it would not grow.

**Reader 2** Jesus said, *I am the vine; you are the branches* (John 15:5). He said that those who live in him, while he is in them, will bear much fruit. Apart from him, we can do nothing.

**Reader 1** You will never be able to get fruit from that piece of bark, because it does not have an independent life of its own. It only lived when it was attached to the tree. Without the tree, it dies.

**Reader 2** Jesus cursed a fig-tree because it was not bearing any fruit. *In the morning, as they went along, they saw the fig-tree, withered from the roots. Peter remembered and said to Jesus, 'Rabbi, look! The fig-tree you cursed has withered!'* (Mark 11:12–14,21).

**Reader 1** We are like this bark. When we cut ourselves off from God, we wither and die. When we think we can do things on our own, we find ourselves failing. We look in many places for life, for energy, for strength – yet we need to get our strength from God. As you look at the bark now, remember those times when you have tried to go it alone, or when you have ignored God. Apologise to God for those times, and for anything else that comes to mind.

**Reader 2** *Then the angel showed me the river of the water of life … flowing from the throne of God . . . On each side of the river stood the tree of life, bearing twelve crops of fruit, yielding its fruit every month. And the leaves of the tree are for the healing of the nations* (Revelation 22:1,2).

**Reader 1** Come to the front of the church now. While you are walking, look at the greenery, the living plants. Admire their greenness and beauty. Imagine the life-giving sap flowing through them, and ask God to give you his life-giving Spirit. If you are holding a piece of bark, place it at the foot of the cross as a sign that you want to turn away from the things that make you dead and dry. Come and take a piece of fruit and ask God to help you to bear much fruit, rather than being dry and dead like old bark.

# The red carpet script

When celebrities arrive at parties and film premieres, the red carpet is rolled out for them… a red road for them to travel on… a road that is beautiful, soft, secure, safe, special. Only important people get the red carpet treatment…

But now we are hearing a voice calling to us. Prepare the way… not for a film star, not for a politician… but for God himself to come and visit us…

Yet making this way has its problems. The ground is rough; there are hills and potholes in the way. We need to prepare the ground for God's red carpet… So let's think and pray for a while about how we can prepare our ground for God.

What are the mountains that get in our way? The obstacles which would make a road have to twist and turn? The things which hinder our relationship with God? The worries… guilt… lack of time…

Now think of things which get in the way of our church's relationship with God: such as arguments… lack of love… money worries…

Spend a few moments asking God about how to bring some of those mountains down…

Now spend a few minutes thinking about the valleys or potholes which give God a bumpy ride. What might these symbolise in our lives? Perhaps they are doubts and fears… times when we find it difficult to trust… times when we find it hard to hope for heaven…

What might they be for the whole Church in our nation? Worries about falling numbers… longings for the way things used to be… fear of failure…

Talk to God about some of the things that come to mind when you think of valleys that need to be raised up. Ask God to help raise them up…

Spend a few minutes thinking about rugged places. Your own rough edges… the things you need to work on… your temper… that one thing you keep wishing you didn't do that you end up doing anyway… your sense of helplessness when faced with so much suffering…

Finally, ask God to help you make some resolutions: things you can do as an individual to make your relationship with God better, or make the world a better place. These could be things like prayer… action… love… making time for God.

If you feel comfortable doing so, take a pen and write your resolutions on the red carpet now. All these are things you can do to prepare your heart for God.

> *In the desert prepare*
>     *the way for the LORD;*
> *make straight in the wilderness*
>     *a highway for our God.*
> *Every valley shall be raised up,*
>     *every mountain and hill made low;*
> *the rough ground shall become level,*
>     *the rugged places a plain.*
> *And the glory of the LORD will be revealed,*
>     *and all mankind together will see it.*
> *For the mouth of the LORD has spoken.*   (Isaiah 40:3–5)

If it is a communion service, after you have decorated your red carpet you may wish to process up the carpet to receive the bread and wine. Removing shoes might be good for this, as long as the carpet isn't too slippery, as then the writing won't get spoiled. Also, removing shoes has the added symbolism that the carpet is 'holy ground'.

# The storm script

Close your eyes, and begin to imagine yourself walking along the sea shore in Galilee. It is evening. You can hear the waves lapping along the shore. You can feel the gentle sea breeze, making your hair ruffle around your face. Ahead of you, you can see Jesus. He is walking along the shore, too.

Look at Jesus. Look at his body posture. His walking style. It seems to be laboured, as if he is very tired. Now, he climbs into a boat, and you follow him. You sit down on a rolled-up fishing net. The air is warm and humid. You can smell the salt, the seaweed, the lingering smells of fish. You look around. The other disciples are all tired too, but Jesus is especially tired. It has been a long day of preaching and healing. Some of the disciples nod off, and so does Jesus, lulled by the gentle swaying of the boat in the waves. You can hear the lapping of the water, the flapping of the sails; you can see flickering lights pinpointing the villages by the lake…

Suddenly, a cold blast of air hits you. You realise the waves are beginning to rise. Thick grey clouds are massing overhead and the air tingles. The boat begins to roll… and suddenly an enormous crash of thunder wakes most of the sleeping men. The boat lurches; the waves get higher; spray begins to splash your face… but Jesus sleeps on.

Soon it is as if the sky is throwing everything it can at you. Sheets of rain are pounding the deck, and the boat is leaping wildly from side to side. It is threatening to capsize. The disciples are shouting at each other, and to Andrew at the back of the boat, desperately trying to keep it on course. Everyone is beginning to panic and their voices sound strangled and strained. The rudder slips in Andrew's hands and the boat spins around and around. You are feeling exhausted, sick and dizzy.

At last one of the men shakes the still-sleeping Jesus. 'Master, MASTER! Save us… we're going to drown!' Jesus sits up, the rain running down his cheeks and beard. He shouts to be heard above the wind. 'You've not got much faith, have you! Why are you afraid?'

You shiver from the cold and the embarrassment of the rebuke. You draw your sodden clothes tighter around you. You wait, curious… for you sense something is about to happen…

Jesus stands up. Though the boat is lurching and spinning wildly, the wind is wailing, the rain is coming down in torrents, the deck is awash and the timbers of the mast are creaking loudly… he stands up and shouts: 'Wind! WIND! BE QUIET!'

And… the wind stops. The boat gives another sudden lurch as it is sent tipping down the crest of another wave. 'WAVES! BE CALM!'

And the sea… becomes like glass. All is silent. All is calm. The only sounds that can be heard are the distant echoes of puzzled voices floating across the water from a few houses on the shore and the sharp intakes of breath of the men in the boat. Then, ever so slowly, the wind begins to blow once more… but this time it is a gentle breeze softly caressing the boat towards the shore.

You feel stunned. Disorientated. Then you hear one dazed man say to another, as Jesus curls up to sleep once more, 'Who is he? What sort of person can he be… if even the wind and the waves do as he says?'

# The house plan script

Jesus said, *Trust in God; trust also in me. In my Father's house are many rooms; if it were not so, I would have told you* (John 14:1,2).

There are many rooms in God's house. Room for us all, however we are feeling; whatever place we may feel we are in today. Let's think about some of the rooms in the typical house, and what they might symbolise for us.

**The living room**: a place of ease and comfort; a relaxed, happy place…

**The bedroom**: a place to go when we are tired or ill…

**The bathroom**: sometimes a place where people hide; where they cry; or wash their tears away so that they can face the world once more…

**The dining room**: a place of welcome, with food, friendship and love…

**The kitchen**: often a place of serving; a place of activity, offering hospitality, warmth and welcome…

**The hallway**: the way out of the house, a place of escape, where people go when they want to get away…

Perhaps these rooms might have other symbolic meanings or other thoughts for you. If that is so, please feel free to use your own meanings.

Let's think about some people in the Bible who were in some of those places.

The living room brings to mind Mary and Martha. Mary, in her home in Bethany, just sat at Jesus' feet, listening to every word he had to say; totally relaxed (Luke 10:38–42).

When we think of the bedroom as the place of recovery from sickness, there are many people we could choose. There was Job, who was covered in sores (Job 2:7,8); the paralysed man who had to be taken to Jesus on his sickbed (Luke 5:17–25); the apostles who fell asleep in the garden of Gethsemane (Luke 22:45); or perhaps Jesus himself, fast asleep in the boat while the storms raged all around him (Matthew 8:23,24).

The bathroom reminds us of the psalmist who said, … *tears have been my food day and night* (Psalm 42:3). Or Elijah, when he fled to the desert and prayed that he might die (1 Kings 19:3,4).

When I think of the kitchen I think of Abraham and Sarah excitedly entertaining the three strangers beneath the oaks of Mamre (Genesis 18:1–15) or Jesus and the apostles amazingly feeding the five thousand with so little bread and fish (Mark 6:30–44).

The dining room suggests the Song of Songs to me: *He has taken me to the banquet hall, and his banner over me is love* (Song of Songs 2:4); or the wedding feast at Cana, so full of love and miracles (John 2:1–11).

Finally, we come to the hallway, and the longing for escape. David cried out, *Oh, that I had the wings of a dove! I would fly away and be at rest – I would flee far away …* (Psalm 55:6) or Moses telling Pharoah to *Let my people go!* (Exodus 7:16).

When you have finished reading the script, allow people time to place themselves and people they know on the plan in the rooms where they feel they are at the moment. If the group is small enough, you may want to gather around the plan. With a larger group, group members may need the opportunity to come up in twos and threes to place themselves on the plan.

When we used this activity and had completed our house plan, it was quite moving to realise that while many of us were in different places, yet we were together in the same place worshipping God and (hopefully!) supporting each other through the rougher times.

Allow some time for silent or open prayer for everyone in their different situations, especially those who are feeling tired, ill or suffering in any way. If you use this prayer idea in a communion service, you could lay the plan on the altar or table, using it almost as an altar cloth.

# The house plan

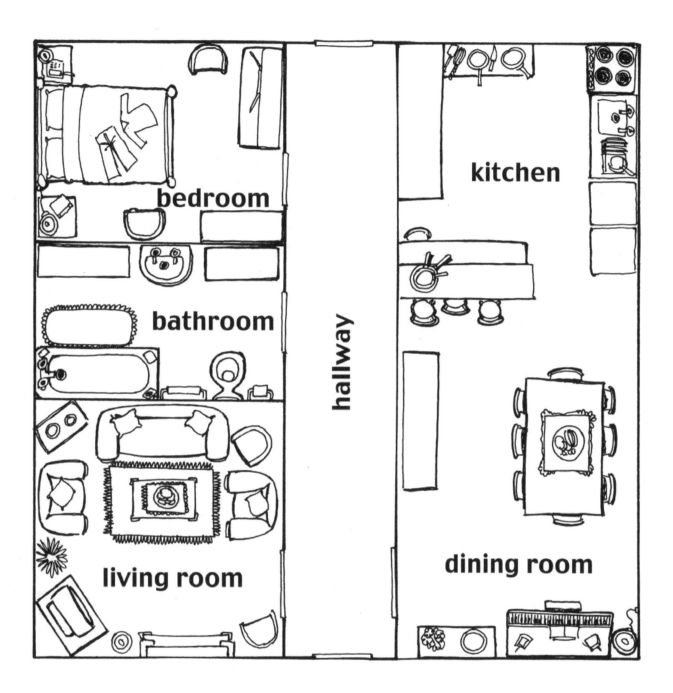

bedroom

kitchen

bathroom

hallway

living room

dining room

# The sour grapes script

Close your eyes and imagine that you are a gardener. And you are searching… travelling many miles to find a good region in which to plant a very particular sort of garden… your personal dream garden.

You look at the detailed weather records for various areas, and eventually opt for a place in the Mediterranean with mild gentle winters, refreshing rain in spring, and beautiful, long hot summers. And then you start trawling the estate agents' ads to find your place… the perfect place… to create your garden.

Finally you find it. You discover the details for an old run-down villa with a vineyard attached. 'Full of rustic charm,' the estate agent says. 'What he meant,' you think, as your foot threatens to crunch through some of the broken floorboards, 'is decrepit!' But by then you have fallen in love with the place. You see its potential. You dream of sitting in a deck chair, surrounded by vines, drinking your first crop of fresh young wine.

Every chance you get, you visit your Mediterranean escape for long weekends and holidays. You follow the advice of all the best D-I-Y programmes… renovating everything… re-pointing bricks, hammering and sawing… chopping and digging… until you collapse into bed with blisters on your hands and an aching back. It takes ages – a good five years to get the place even beginning to look right. But in the end, it's a home and a garden to be proud of… the restored walls, the carefully-tended earth, the stone fountain that splashes so sweetly, the young green vines trailing on their new trellises. Each time you visit, the vines are a little more mature, beginning to look so ripe, so delicious.

Finally the day comes when you can make your first batch of grape juice. You pour it into a glass jug, and watch the light sparkle through the liquid. You sniff the perfume of newly pressed fruit, and then you taste.

Yeugh! Sour grapes!

The disappointment is tremendous. You sit and think about the hours, the days, the years of work, the calluses on your hands. Your dreams for the future crumble. This was your wonderful garden! You collapse in a heap… and weep. This vineyard has taken every penny you had… every ounce of your strength and energy.

Later, you dry your eyes, wash your face, and determine to find some explanation. Why has it all gone so terribly wrong? You spend hours scouring the library and the Internet looking for an answer.

But when you find an answer, it leaves you still more depressed. For the land you bought is situated too near a site where a chemical factory was active a decade ago. The land is poisoned. Your hopes of a harvest are gone forever. As you sit and stare at the report you have found in the library, you remember echoes of a similar story; a tale of God who called Israel his vineyard and Judah his vines. God… tending his vines through history, spending centuries nurturing a garden planet in which to place people, breathing life into them when the time was right. God tended them and taught them. But the fruit was sour. The people turned their backs on him and practiced murder and hate.

Remembering their victims' cry for justice and God's despair over the way the fruit has turned out, you bury your head in your hands and weep again, this time shedding tears for other poisoned vines. You cry for the children in Iraq whose homes have been destroyed… (pause); you cry for the lost potential of those who have died of AIDS in South Africa… (pause); you weep for all the vineyards that have become war zones… (pause).

Here you can insert other relevant topical examples of 'sour fruit' around the world.

You weep for all the dreams destroyed… and your cry becomes a prayer. For mercy. For God to rebuild this broken world.

# The fire and water script

Jesus promised that he would give us living water. He said that whoever drinks the water he gives will never be thirsty again. He said that the water he gives would become a spring of water welling up to eternal life. His invitation to all who are thirsty is to come and drink. His promise is that they will experience streams of living water flowing from within them... by which, says John, he meant the Spirit who would be given to believers.

Look at the water... see the ripples through the glass. The water acts like a lens, magnifying the world around. Think about the purity of the water, its clarity.

Lord, give us the living water of your Spirit... so that we can cause ripples of your love and life to spread to everyone around us... Open our eyes to see the world your way, though the lens of your love... Give us your purity... your clarity...

Next, pour some olive oil on the water.

> You prepare a table before me
> > in the presence of my enemies.
> You anoint my head with oil;
> > my cup overflows.
> Surely goodness and love will follow me
> > all the days of my life,
> and I will dwell in the house of the LORD
> > for ever.

You anoint us with the oil of your Spirit... soothing us... healing us... providing for us... Send your healing Spirit on us now... calm our troubled lives.

Next put the wick holder and the wick on top of the oil on the water and continue reading the script (Acts 2:1–4) slowly and with frequent pauses.

> When the day of Pentecost came, they were all together in one place. Suddenly a sound like the blowing of a violent wind came from heaven and filled the whole house where they were sitting. They saw what seemed to be tongues of fire that separated and came to rest of each of them. All of them were filled with the Holy Spirit...

Then light the wick of the oil lamp, before continuing.

Send us the fire of your Spirit... light us up where we are dark inside... fire us up with the warmth of your love where we have become cold and uncaring... Come, Holy Spirit, and fill us...

# The Lazarus script

You see a graveyard, with a number of tombs cut into the hillside. Some distance away, there is a house with a huge crowd of people milling around it. You see Martha, running out of the house and along the road to meet a man. It's Jesus.

You watch as Martha embraces Jesus. She is crying. In fact, her red-rimmed eyes tell you she has been crying for some time. Jesus is speaking to her, standing tall as if what he is saying has deep significance. Then you see Martha running back to the house and coming out again, this time with her sister Mary.

The crowd near the house follow her and surround Jesus. What's going on? You see Mary fall at Jesus' feet. She is crying, her hands covering her face. Tears are also running down Jesus' face. Mary stands and points towards one particular tomb and now all three of them are walking towards the hillside.

You see Jesus pointing, gesturing at the stone covering the entrance to the tomb. Other figures seem to remonstrate with him, shaking their heads. Several people close to the stone cover their faces with the wide sleeves of their robes. Are they covering their eyes? No, they are covering their noses.

Then two hefty-looking men heave the huge rock away from the tomb's entrance. The crowd take several steps back. Jesus is raising his hands, looking up into heaven. Then you see Jesus make a slow beckoning gesture towards the tomb.

Everything seems to stand still for few seconds. Then... your heart misses a beat... a figure staggers out of the tomb, stumbling because he is wrapped in strips of cloth, some of which cover his face so that he can't see. Lazarus is alive!

Now ask everyone to relax for a few seconds to prepare themselves for using their imagination with a second sense: hearing. Again, tell them they are bystanders in positions where they can pick up everything that's said.

The first thing that strikes you is the loud wailing and weeping sounds coming from Martha and Mary's house. Then you hear footsteps running along the road. When they stop you hear Martha's voice, which sounds bitter and angry.

'Lord, if only you had been here, my brother would not have died!'

Then, with a little hope in her voice. 'Yet – even now – I know God will give you whatever you ask.'

Next, you hear the voice of Jesus: slower, kind, gentle.

'Your brother will rise again.'

Martha's reply is slowed by sobs. 'I know he will rise again – in the resurrection at the last day.'

Jesus raises his voice now; it is strong, purposeful. 'I am the resurrection and the life. Anyone who believes in me will live, even though he dies. And anyone who believes in me will never die. Do you believe this?'

Martha's voice is a little lighter as she replies, 'I believe that you are the Christ, the Son of God, who was promised.'

Her footsteps return along the road; and you hear her calling her sister. 'Mary! Mary! The teacher is here!'

More footsteps as the two women return to Jesus. Mary speaks in a soft voice: 'Lord, if only you had been here, Lazarus would still be alive.' As she speaks she collapses, sobbing, into the dust at the feet of Jesus.

Next you hear deep painful sobs from Jesus himself.

'Where have you laid his body?'

'Come and see, Lord.'

Others have arrived, because you hear more voices now over the sounds of weeping.

'See how he loved him!' You pick out the amazed comment from one bystander. But another, harsh and cynical, is complaining loudly that Jesus, if he was a healer, should have been able to keep his friend from dying.

'Take the stone away!' Jesus raises his voice commandingly above the gathering hubbub.

Some start to protest. And Martha appeals, 'Lord, think of the smell! He's already been in the tomb for four days.'

But the authority and even impatience in Jesus' voice cannot be denied.

'Didn't I tell you that, if you believed, you would see the glory of God!'

You hear the grinding noise of the stone being pushed away with some effort from the tomb entrance; the men doing the shifting are grunting and panting.

Then you hear Jesus praying – a prayer not of petition or sorrow but of thanks.

Then, taking a deep breath, Jesus calls out, in a huge voice that seems to hang in the air and make the stones tremble.

'Lazarus, come out!'

Silence. Then a sharp intake of breath from several in the crowd, followed by footsteps. Someone lets out a stifled scream. Then there are growing murmurs of amazement. You hear shouts, a few muttered phrases from the psalms, some whoops of incredulous delight. Lazarus is alive!

Now allow everyone to relax for a few seconds before exploring using a third sense: smell.

There are all the usual rich smells of a village in springtime: early flowers, grass, trees. But as you move toward Martha and Mary's house you pick up different scents. You can smell the sweat of a crowd and behind it the lingering scent of funeral spices: myrrh and aloes.

When Jesus shouts for the stone to be rolled away, you reel with the appalling smell of decay that comes from the tomb, so strong it almost makes you gag. But when Jesus commands Lazarus to come out, the smell of decay that was so stifling suddenly melts away, leaving just a lingering aftertaste, and the pungent aroma of Eastern spices. Lazarus is alive!

Now move onto the fourth sense: taste. There are no tastes mentioned specifically in the story, but we might be able to surmise some.

As you become one of the mourners, you taste the refreshments laid on for you to eat and drink. There's fresh bread, wine, water and olives.

As Mary, you find your appetite has disappeared; all you can taste is your own dry mouth, though sometimes you can taste the salt from your many tears. The taste of the air from the tomb when it's opened is evil, but then again there is the dry mouth of anticipation. As you embrace your brother you taste the remains of embalming spices of his cheek. Lazarus is alive!

Now turn to the fifth sense: touch.

As Martha, you grab hold of the old wooden door, open it and run. You can feel the hot sand slipping into your sandals, the dust of the road clouding around your ankles. You greet Jesus with the customary kiss on the cheek, feeling his face hot from the journey. You grasp his hand while you are talking, then reluctantly let him go while you fetch your sister.

As Mary, you run to Jesus, tears on your cheeks. You fall at his feet, grabbing at his ankles. The sand you kneel on is scorching hot. Jesus pulls you to your feet with his gentle hands, and you walk together to the tomb, each step feeling heavy, sad.

As Martha, you touch Jesus' arm when he commands the stone to be rolled away, trying to hold back his beckoning arm.

As one of the men, you reach out to the huge rock, rough and almost unbearably hot after a morning in the sun. You search for a good handhold and heave with a force that makes your whole body shake. The stone moves slowly, grazing your palm. When Jesus cries out to Lazarus, you feel your whole body shake with the force of his cry. And when Lazarus comes out, you feel your heart leap with fright to see a supposedly dead man standing in front of you. Your heart beating wildly, you begin to help release him from the strips of cloth. Beneath the cloth, stiffened with the sticky ointments used for embalming, you become aware of the warmth of a living human body. You touch his chest, feel the ribs rising, the muscles tensing. Lazarus is not a ghost. Lazarus is alive!

# The man on the stretcher script

We're going to imagine we were actually there when Jesus healed this paralysed man. Get into a comfortable position, close your eyes and ask God's Holy Spirit to come and speak to you, teaching you new things…

You are the owner of a house in Capernaum where Jesus is staying for a time. He has been away for a while, but has just returned. How do you feel when Jesus comes in the door after being away?

Soon after his return, quite a lot of people begin to gather at the house. What is your reaction?

So many are arriving that after a while the living space is packed, and quite a crowd are standing around the open door.

What are you thinking now? What are you feeling? Where are you standing? Outside? If so, see if you can just squeeze inside the door.

Then Jesus begins to preach… You have heard from others about many wonderful things he has been saying to the crowds as he has been travelling. Now you are hearing him for yourself. Blessed are the poor in spirit, he says, for theirs is the kingdom of heaven… Blessed are those who mourn, for they will be comforted… Blessed are the meek, for they will inherit the earth…

How does it feel to hear those things, for the very first time, from the lips of Jesus himself?

Glancing behind, you catch sight of some men carrying someone on a stretcher. It's just a rough mat made of woven rushes slung between two poles. They are trying to get through the crowd at the doorway, but they can't make it.

What do you think about the men and their disabled friend?

After a few fruitless minutes they disappear. Time passes while you and the crowd go on listening to Jesus, amazed at the things he is saying.

Then slowly you become aware of some strange scraping and scratching sounds coming from somewhere above your head. You see little clouds of clay dust falling from the roof. What's going on? You realise that some kind of opening in the roof is being worked on. What is your reaction?

Soon the opening is large enough to see a patch of blue sky though it. You recognise the men working on the roof – they're the stretcher-bearers. Now, they are beginning to lower the mat down through the opening. What are you thinking?

Has Jesus noticed? What's his face tell you about what he's thinking?

Jesus is looking at the paralysed man now that he has been lowered to the ground at his feet. After all you've heard about Jesus you are expecting him to say, 'Get up, you are healed.' But you hear him say, 'Son, your sins are forgiven.'

What? How strange! What do you think? What is everyone else's reaction?

You look around. A small group you recognise as teachers from the local synagogue are looking shocked and uncomfortable. They turn to each other and start muttering. Several others are looking confused; some are looking hostile; others rather intrigued.

'Why are you thinking that?' Jesus' words are challenging, and he's mostly looking at the religious teachers.

'I want you to know that I have the authority to forgive sins.'

Then he looks again at the man at his feet.

'Get up off your stretcher and walk home.'

And the paralysed man does just that. You see him stand, see him walk away… you see him with your own eyes.

The crowd part to let the man through, carrying his stretcher mat with him. Some have started to shout praises to God. Others are dumbfounded, shaking their heads in amazement. What is your reaction?

You may want to stop at this point and encourage people to share their thoughts in twos or threes; or ask them to jot down their thoughts for sharing later.

Now encourage everyone to get themselves comfortable once more, to close their eyes and ask God to speak to them again.

Now imagine you are one of the paralysed man's four friends. How do you feel about your friend's disability? What happened earlier today to make you and the others set out to bring him to Jesus? Why were you so determined to see him?

Now you are arriving near the house, helping to carry your friend on the stretcher. It's impossible to get through the crowd. Everyone wants to get as close to Jesus as they can. How do you feel? Will you give up and go home?

Then you spot the staircase up to the roof. How easy is it to get the stretcher up there? And what do you plan to do next? How do you think everyone else is going to react to your plan?

How difficult is it to make the opening in the roof? And to lower your friend through?

Now he's safely resting on the ground at Jesus' feet. But nothing seems to be happening. Jesus is talking to the group of men from the synagogue. How do you feel?

At last Jesus is talking to your friend. As you look down you see him get shakily to his feet – and start to walk. Was this what you were expecting? How do you feel? What do you do next?

Again, you may want to conclude with a short time when people can share their thoughts and insights.

# The feathers script

**Reader 1**   Take your feather and put it on the ground at your feet. Admire its beauty… the intricacy of the vanes… the strong stem of the quill. Then crouch down and push it with your finger. How does it move? Does it move far? Probably not. Imagine that you are that feather. Alone, abandoned on the ground, unable to fly… Tell God about the times when you have felt like that recently… helpless… powerless… or far from God.

**Reader 2**   *Then he said to me, 'Prophesy to the breath; prophesy, son of man, and say to it, "This is what the Sovereign LORD says: Come from the four winds, O breath, and breathe into these slain, that they may live"'* (Ezekiel 37:9).

**Reader 1**   Take your feather and place it in your palm. Now blow… Watch the feather fly from your hand and drift gently to the ground. Pick up your feather and repeat the experience… See how the wind of your breath supports the feather… lifting it… helping it fly.

**Reader 2**   *…the LORD God formed the man from the dust of the ground and breathed into his nostrils the breath of life, and the man became a living being* (Genesis 2:7).

**Reader 1**   The twelfth-century Abbess Hildegard told a story of a king sitting on a throne. He stooped down, picked up a feather from the ground, and ordered it to fly. It did fly, but not because of any strength or ability of its own. It flew because the breath of the king moved it. I am like this, too. A feather on the breath of God…

**Reader 2**   *Jesus said, 'Peace be with you! As the Father has sent me, I am sending you.' And with that he breathed on them and said, 'Receive the Holy Spirit'* (John 20:21,22).

**Reader 1**   Imagine once again you are that feather… breathe upon it once more… and as you do, ask God to breathe on you with his Holy Spirit. As the feather floats to the ground, ask God to guide you in right directions… and ask him to reach deep inside all those situations where you feel powerless or helpless, to allow his power to work through you. If you feel you can, give him permission to come into those areas to work.

**Reader 2**   *Suddenly a sound like the blowing of a violent wind came from heaven and filled the whole house where they were sitting. They saw what seemed to be tongues of fire that separated and came to rest on each of them. All of them were filled with the Holy Spirit…* (Acts 2:2–4).

**Reader 1**   Breathe on me, breath of God:

    fill me with life anew,

that as you love, so I may love,

    and do what you would do.

© Jubilate Hymns

# Smell trail script 1: Mary anoints Jesus with perfume

**(installation: a dish of perfume and perfume bottle) from John 12:1–8**

Close your eyes and imagine that you are in a house in Bethany, a small village on the outskirts of the city of Jerusalem. You are at dinner, and Jesus is the guest of honour. Martha is bustling around, serving the meal and making sure the guests are supplied with wine. Lazarus, Martha's brother, is reclining at the table with Jesus.

Then you see another woman come into the room. You recognise her as Mary, the sister of Martha and Lazarus. She is carrying something in a pot. You sense her pause… steeling herself for a moment, then watch as she runs to Jesus and falls at his feet, deliberately breaking the perfume bottle.

As you watch, the perfume pours out, all over Jesus' feet… flowing, flowing… looking for a moment as if it will never stop. The entire house fills with the smell of the strong perfume – beautiful, exotic and precious. It's pure nard: the most expensive perfume of all.

Someone stands. It is Judas Iscariot, one of Jesus' disciples. He is angry. He complains about the disgusting waste of money. It could have been used to help the poor. He's got a good point, but you sense something in his voice… an edge of selfish greed, perhaps? You watch expectantly to see what Jesus is going to say in reply. Is he going to agree with Judas and be irritated with Mary?

Jesus turns and shouts at Judas, 'Leave her alone!' Then, softly and sadly now, he adds, 'It was intended that she should save this perfume for the day of my burial. You will always have the poor among you, but you will not always have me.'

Imagine that you are Mary. How does it feel to have taken your most precious possession and poured it out over the feet of Jesus?

Now think about your own most precious possessions. Do you ever give them to Jesus?

When you have finished, re-wind this tape for the next person.


# Smell trail script 2: The cleansing of the Temple

**(installation: frankincense or frankincense oil behind some sort of safety guard) from Matthew 21:1–14**

Close your eyes and imagine that you are in the bustling city of Jerusalem, not far from the Temple. The crowds who have journeyed to Jerusalem for the Passover festival seem to be behaving strangely. They have lined the road for some sort of procession, enthusiastically waving palm branches. You can hear words being chanted and you gradually pick out 'Hosanna' and 'Blessed is he who comes in the name of the Lord'.

Now, surrounded by more people, a man is making his way up the hill, riding a donkey.

Nearer the Temple, there is a buzz of conversation. People are asking, 'Who is this man?' 'It's Jesus,' someone shouts. 'You know, the prophet from Nazareth in Galilee.'

You move closer to the entrance to the Temple. What is this prophet going to do? He strides into the courtyard, which reeks of incense, animals and the blood of sacrifices. You are unprepared for what happens next. Jesus overturns the tables of the moneychangers and those who are selling doves. And then he shouts, 'My house will be called a house of prayer, but you are making it a den of robbers!'

People start running in all directions and for a while there is a terrible commotion. Animals are bolting everywhere and some people dive under the tables to try and snatch up some of the spilt money.

But then a strange silence descends over the place, as if somehow Jesus has made the place sacred once more.

Quietly, blind and lame beggars are limping slowly towards Jesus. He stretches out his hands… and they are healed!

Stretch out your hands now as if you want to meet those healing hands of Jesus…. Who or what would you like Jesus to heal today? You can ask for healing for yourself, or for someone else you know who desperately needs a touch from Jesus…

When you have finished, re-wind the tape for the next person.

# Smell trail script 3: Jesus washes his disciples' feet

### (installation: a bowl of soapy water) from John 13:1–15

Close your eyes, and imagine that you are in the upper room with Jesus' disciples. They are just starting to serve the evening meal when you see Jesus get up from his place and take off his outer robe. He wraps a towel around his waist, and you wonder what he is going to do next. You watch as he pours water into a basin. Then he begins to wash the feet of the nearest disciple.

You feel a profound sense of shock. This is all wrong! Jesus is supposed to be the master. The servant is supposed to do the footwashing. Or the newest disciple. Not Jesus. Each man seems to accept the situation uneasily, until Jesus gets to Simon Peter. You hear him protest.

'No. You'll never wash my feet!'

Jesus replies, 'If I don't wash you, you won't belong to me.'

'Then wash not just my feet, but my head and hands as well,' says Simon Peter.

Jesus replies that Peter is clean enough and so has no need for extra washing. But then adds something about not everyone being clean. You see him glance across the room at one of the other disciples.

When he has washed the feet of all the disciples, Jesus replaces his robe and returns to his place. Once more he looks like the teacher, and not a domestic slave. He announces, 'Now that I, the one you call "Lord" and "Teacher", have washed your feet, you also should wash one another's feet. I have given you an example to follow.'

Think about what that command of Jesus could mean for you today… Probably he does not require you to wash anyone's feet. But perhaps he wants you to help someone, or to do some task that everyone else finds difficult? What footwashing is Jesus asking from you?

When you have finished, re-wind the tape for the next person.

# Smell trail script 4: The Passover meal

### (installation: herbs, bread, wine and lamb) from Matthew 26:20–29

Close your eyes and imagine that you are in the upper room with the other disciples, sharing the Passover meal together: unleavened bread, bitter herbs, wine and the Passover lamb.

Suddenly you are filled with fear, as Jesus utters a terrible prophecy: 'I tell you the truth, one of you will betray me … '

Your first awful thought is that it might be you and you imagine that everyone else is thinking the same.

Then, one by one, everyone starts protesting, 'Surely, you don't mean me!' Jesus explains that it is indeed someone around the table, eating with him. You see Jesus dip his bread into the bowl of lamb – and at the same moment Judas dips his bread too. Is that just coincidence? You are shocked to the core… how could someone so close to

Jesus… someone who has been with him for three amazing years… walking and talking on the journey with them all…

No! It isn't possible!

But there are more shocks to come. Jesus takes a piece of bread and breaks it, saying, 'Take and eat; this is my body.' The unleavened bread cracks ominously, with a grisly echo. You are filled with terror at the thought of Jesus being torn apart in the way that he just broke that bread. Then he gives pieces of the bread to everyone. He gives his bread, his broken body, to you. And you don't understand. But you know somehow that something incredibly important is happening. You search your mind, trying to read the meaning in it all. It fills you with such dread.

Next, Jesus lifts up a cup of blood-red wine. You hear him say, 'All of you, drink some of this. This is my blood of the covenant, my blood poured out for many for the forgiveness of sins.' He passes around the cup to us to drink, just as he gave us the bread. I can't take it in. A broken body? Spilt blood? How is this going to happen? He tells us to eat the bread and drink the wine to remember him. But why? How could we forget him?

Take a few minutes now to thank Jesus for the incredible gift he gave us: his own body, broken on the Cross, to rescue us from the death penalty of our sins…

When you have finished, re-wind the tape for the next person.

# Smell trail script 5: The Mount of Olives

### (installation: olives, olive oil in hot water) from Luke 22:39–46

Close your eyes and imagine that you have followed Jesus to the Mount of Olives. He says to you, 'Pray for strength against temptation.' You watch him as he moves a stone's throw away, kneels and prays, 'Father, if you are willing, take this cup from me; yet not my will, but yours be done.'

The other disciples, weary after the exhausting and terrible events of that evening, begin to close their eyes, nod and fall asleep. But you keep your eyes on Jesus, hearing him cry out to God in deep agony. He is sweating profusely, and you notice with horror that his sweat is becoming bloody. Even more amazing, you see what you feel must be an angel appear from heaven, who seems to be shielding the crumpled body of Jesus. Then, looking stronger, Jesus rises and walks over to the other disciples. He cries out, waking them, and tells them to get up and pray… but by then there is no more time!

Suddenly a crowd appears, led by… Judas! He stops in front of Jesus and kisses him. Now you know. This is the moment of supreme betrayal. Jesus is arrested and led away…

Sometimes it's easy to look on from our place of safety and criticise the disciples for falling asleep, for running away, for not being strong. Yet we, too, are incredibly weak.

Spend some time now talking to God about some of the weaknesses you see in yourself.

When you are ready, re-wind the tape for the next person.

# Smell trail script 6: Peter denies Jesus

**(installation: metal bowl or barbecue with ashes – protected if necessary) from Luke 22:54–62**

Close your eyes and imagine that you are sitting by a fire, warming your hands. You are in the courtyard of the high priest, watching a serving girl in conversation with a man. You are drawn to the scene because the man is obviously trying – rather unsuccessfully – to hide his face inside his hood.

The girl is looking closely at Peter and you hear her say, quite loudly, 'This man was with him. With that Jesus who has just been arrested.'

Peter tries to dismiss her. 'Woman, I don't know him!'

Peter shrinks again into his hood, trying to make himself look smaller. But now someone else points at him and insists, 'I recognise you. You were one of them!'

You wonder if Peter is thinking of admitting it. But then you see him frown and say, 'You're mistaken. I am not one of them.'

The man shrugs, almost as if he knows Peter is lying. The people around the fire go back to their gossip. An hour passes… a long hour… during which you wonder about Jesus, being held somewhere else in the building… suffering questioning and beatings.

Then you hear another accusing voice and see another pointing finger being directed straight at Peter. 'You are definitely one of the Jesus band.'

Peter shouts something unprintable in response, adding, 'I just don't know what you're talking about!'

Even as he is saying these words, we hear the crowing of a cock. It is close to morning. Jesus is being bustled out of the high priest's house under guard and, as the little group passes through the courtyard, Jesus turns and looks straight at Peter.

Peter stands, runs from the courtyard, his eyes brimming with tears. You follow, watching as he collapses in a heap near the outer wall, now crying bitterly, his shoulders shaking with great sobs…

We live in a society in which it can be hard to admit that you not only believe in God but try to live a Christian lifestyle.

Pray now for people who are finding it really tough because of bullying or because they are being pressured into doing wrong things. And remember people in different countries around the world who find themselves in terrible danger, imprisoned or tortured because of their faith.

When you have finished, re-wind the tape for the next person.


# Smell trail script 7: Jesus on the Cross

**(installation: cup of vinegar) from Luke 23:33–46**

Close your eyes and imagine that you are standing at the foot of the Cross. You can smell many terrible smells: there is blood and sweat and nameless rotting substances mingling to create an overwhelming stench of decay.

And in the midst of it all is Jesus…

Jesus is saying, 'Father, forgive them. They don't know what they are doing.'

He is dying… slowly and in agony. If he can forgive those crucifying him, can he forgive you, too? You tell him some of those things for which you desperately need forgiveness. When he turns to look at you, you know you are clean.

Near the end, a soldier runs to get a sponge on which they offer Jesus a few drops of wine vinegar. A couple of other soldiers are muttering together about the possibility of Elijah coming to save him.

Then you hear Jesus' last terrible cry and watch him take his last breath. The world is plunged into darkness. You feel the earth literally shake, and watch, terrified, as rocks split open. From the Temple Mount there is shrieking, and the rumour that is being spread is that the huge temple veil has been torn in two, from top to bottom, leaving the Holy of Holies open wide.

When you have finished, re-wind the tape for the next person.

# Smell trail script 8: Jesus is buried

### (installation: myrrh oil and possibly aloe vera in a pot of hot water) from John 19:38–42

Close your eyes and imagine that you are at the foot of the Cross. The limp, scarred body is being taken down. Two wealthy-looking men step forward from the shadows. You recognise them as Joseph of Arimathea and Nicodemus. Nicodemus has a number of his servants with him, carrying myrrh, aloes and strips of linen. You can smell the rich pungency of the spices above the general smell of blood, sweat and decay.

They move very quickly. The sun is about to set and the Sabbath to begin. They carry Jesus to a fresh tomb cut into the rocky hillside and you watch as they wrap Jesus in the strips of cloth.

You can't help thinking about how terrible this funeral is. Such haste. No eulogies. No songs. Just two or three mourners. The wrapping complete and the body laid on its ledge, the huge stone is rolled over the entrance and everyone leaves. It begins to sink in that Jesus has died. Really died…

Think about anyone you know who has lost someone they cared about recently. Ask Jesus to come and meet them, as one who knows what it is to suffer and die.

When you have finished, re-wind the tape for the next person.

# Smell trail script 9: A meal on the beach

### (installation: a pan of freshly fried fish) from John 21:1–14

Close your eyes and picture yourself standing by the Sea of Tiberias. It is early morning, and the pale sun glints on the waves. Not far from the shore, you see the disciples in a boat, fishing. They look tired and depressed. They've obviously caught nothing all night.

Then you see Jesus nearby and he yells at them to cast their net on the other side of the boat. They do so – and find such a large number of fish in their net that they are unable to haul it into the boat properly.

Next, you see an excited Simon Peter jump out of the boat and wade for the shore to see Jesus. The others bring the boat in and land the fish.

Pretty soon there is a small fire burning, with fish and bread on it. It smells amazing! Jesus has cooked them breakfast. He is not a ghost – but is a person who once was dead and now is alive… someone who can cook fish for his friends, someone who can sit down and eat with them. Jesus has risen from the dead!

Talk to Jesus right now, knowing that you are talking to someone who is alive… someone who knows your deepest thoughts and hears your every word. Remember to express your thanks to him for all the marvellous things he has done for you…

When you have finished, re-wind the tape for the next person.

# The Lazarus meal

**Time**: the night after Lazarus has been raised from the dead

**Place**: Lazarus' house in Bethany

**Characters**: Lazarus, Mary, Martha, Simon Peter, John, Judas Iscariot, a Pharisee, Andrew, Thomas

**Character briefings:**

✂ ─ ─ ─ ─ ─ ─ ─ ─ ─ ─ ─ ─ ─ ─ ─ ─ ─ ─ ─ ─ ─ ─ ─ ─ ─ ─ ─ ─ ─ ─ ─ ─ ─ ─ ─ ─

**Lazarus**  Lived in Bethany, a village on the eastern slope of the Mount of Olives, about two miles from Jerusalem. Was dead until yesterday lunchtime, when he was raised by Jesus. Had been dead four days, having suffered a sudden illness (see John 11). Has two sisters, Mary and Martha. Has suffered death threats since his resurrection (John 12:10).

✂ ─ ─ ─ ─ ─ ─ ─ ─ ─ ─ ─ ─ ─ ─ ─ ─ ─ ─ ─ ─ ─ ─ ─ ─ ─ ─ ─ ─ ─ ─ ─ ─ ─ ─ ─ ─

**Mary**  Lives in Bethany. Anointed (or is soon to anoint) Jesus with her expensive perfume. Has a sister called Martha and a brother called Lazarus who has just been raised from the dead. Likes to sit at Jesus' feet listening to everything he says. When Lazarus died and she saw Jesus she fell at his feet weeping (John 11:32). Martha seems to be the one nominally in charge of the household. Maybe she's older than Mary? (see Luke 10:38–41).

✂ ─ ─ ─ ─ ─ ─ ─ ─ ─ ─ ─ ─ ─ ─ ─ ─ ─ ─ ─ ─ ─ ─ ─ ─ ─ ─ ─ ─ ─ ─ ─ ─ ─ ─ ─ ─

**Martha**  Lives in Bethany. Opened her home to Jesus, so seems to be nominally in charge of it for some reason. Maybe she's the oldest? Maybe she's the bossiest? Has a sister called Mary who likes to sit at Jesus' feet (see Luke 10:38–41) and a brother called Lazarus who has just been raised from the dead. Martha is hardworking and likes to prepare things properly. She criticises her sister for not helping sometimes. Martha is the one to greet Jesus first when he visits them after Lazarus has died (John 11:20).

✂ ─ ─ ─ ─ ─ ─ ─ ─ ─ ─ ─ ─ ─ ─ ─ ─ ─ ─ ─ ─ ─ ─ ─ ─ ─ ─ ─ ─ ─ ─ ─ ─ ─ ─ ─ ─

**Simon Peter**  Simon is the first disciple to say that Jesus is the Christ; for this he gets the nickname Peter – a rock. He feels deeply unworthy when he first meets Jesus and Jesus gives him a miraculous catch of fish (Luke 5:8). His mother-in-law is healed by Jesus. He is sometimes immensely enthusiastic, but doesn't always think things through (see John 13:9 and Mark 9:5). With James and John, he was one of the disciples closest to Jesus. Later in the Gospel narratives he cuts off a soldier's ear (John 18:10).

✂ ─ ─ ─ ─ ─ ─ ─ ─ ─ ─ ─ ─ ─ ─ ─ ─ ─ ─ ─ ─ ─ ─ ─ ─ ─ ─ ─ ─ ─ ─ ─ ─ ─ ─ ─ ─

**John**  Originally a fisherman, his father was called Zebedee (see Matthew 4:21). Astonished by Jesus at first (Luke 5:10). He is also known as 'the disciple Jesus loved'. He wanted to sit at Jesus' side with his brother James (see Mark 10:37). Ambitious perhaps? He wanted to call down fire from heaven on one occasion! (Luke 9:54). But he also had his spiritual side and was a deep thinker, judging by his writings (see John's Gospel and the letters 1, 2, 3 John).

**Character briefings:**

✂ — — — — — — — — — — — — — — — — — — — — — — — — — — — — — — — — —

**Judas Iscariot** The son of Simon Iscariot, Judas is one of the 12 apostles, and the one who betrayed Jesus for 30 pieces of silver (Matthew 26:14). Later threw the money into the temple and went and hanged himself. Objected to Mary anointing Jesus' feet with perfume as the money could have been sold and given to the poor. Though keeper of the money bag, he was a thief and used to help himself to what was there (John 12:4–6).

✂ — — — — — — — — — — — — — — — — — — — — — — — — — — — — — — — — —

**Andrew** He was a fisherman and lived with his brother Simon Peter and Simon Peter's family (Mark 1:29,30). Together with Peter, James and John, he asks Jesus when the Temple will be torn down (Mark 13:3). Andrew is the one who introduces Peter to Jesus. He overhears what John the Baptist has said about him, follows Jesus, then goes and tells his brother that he thinks he has found the Christ (John 1:40,41). He is also the one to make the (crazy?) suggestion about a boy with five loaves and two fishes at the feeding of the five thousand (John 6:9). Andrew also tells Jesus when some Greeks come to see him (John 12:22). Was he therefore acting as some sort of PA/receptionist?

✂ — — — — — — — — — — — — — — — — — — — — — — — — — — — — — — — — —

**Pharisee** The Pharisees were Jewish teachers of the Law. Jesus makes many criticisms of them because they do not obey the spirit of the Law while trying to obey its letter strictly (see Matthew 23:1–36 for a detailed description of what Jesus said against them). Shortly after Lazarus was raised, some people reported what had happened to the Pharisees who, together with the chief priests, called a meeting of the Sanhedrin, plotting against Jesus. The Pharisees sometimes tried to trap Jesus (see Matthew 22:15–17).

✂ — — — — — — — — — — — — — — — — — — — — — — — — — — — — — — — — —

**Thomas** When the rest of the disciples are worried about Jesus visiting so close to Jerusalem so soon after the Jews had tried to stone him, Thomas says, 'Let us also go, that we may die with him' (see John 11:8,16). Thomas is sometimes called 'the twin' – maybe he had a twin brother? Thomas is also famous for doubting that Jesus was risen at first, until he'd actually touched his scars (John 20:24-29). He has an enquiring mind, as he asks, 'Lord, we don't know where you're going, so how can we know the way?' (John 14:5).

✂ — — — — — — — — — — — — — — — — — — — — — — — — — — — — — — — — —

# Quote cards

| | |
|---|---|
| I don't believe it! | I hate you. |
| I think I'm in love. | Suddenly, everything's changed... |
| I blame the parents... | He should be arrested. |
| He hates me! | They're all crazy! |
| I'm terrified. | Why don't you leave me alone? |
| I can't stand the pain... | They say it's hopeless... |
| Don't leave me! | You've got to help... |
| I just want to know the truth. | I don't get it! |
| What's going on? | It's so unfair! |
| Why? | You're so wonderful! |
| Put him in charge! | OK... I'll help. |
| I'll kill him! | I don't know what to do. |
| Don't talk to me! | Get me out of here! |
| You don't understand... | No! I'm not! |
| I feel so dirty... | We're desperate... |

# The Exodus journey meditations

These are given here as they might be for photocopied signposts, but they could alternatively be recorded for listening to at each station.

---

### 1 The burning bush

*… Moses was tending the flock of Jethro his father-in-law … There the angel of the LORD appeared to him in flames of fire from within a bush … God called to him from within the bush, 'Moses! Moses!'… The LORD said, 'I have indeed seen the misery of my people in Egypt. I have heard them crying out because of their slave drivers, and I am concerned about their suffering. So I have come down to rescue them from the hand of the Egyptians'* (from Exodus 3:1–8).

This was the start of a journey for Moses – a calling from God, the beginning of a task he had to accomplish. We may never see anything as spectacular as a burning bush, or a bright light on the road like the apostle Paul did, but we are all called by God to do things for him… Great things or little things… all are important.

Think about things you know God has called you to, and pray about them. Perhaps you need help with what he has called you to do. Perhaps you are unsure about God's calling to you. Give thanks for the things he has helped you accomplish, or spend a few minutes asking him to make the next step of the journey clear for you.

---

### 2 Trapped!

*… Moses and Aaron went to Pharaoh and said, 'This is what the LORD, the God of Israel, says: Let my people go … That same day Pharaoh gave this order to the slave drivers and foremen in charge of the people: 'You are no longer to supply the people with straw for making bricks; let them go and gather their own straw. But require them to make the same number of bricks as before; don't reduce the quota. They are lazy; that is why they are crying out, "Let us go and sacrifice to our God". Make the work harder…'* (from Exodus 5:1–9).

This passage epitomises the cruelty of slavery. Moses was trying to persuade Pharaoh to free the people and the ruler responded by making the conditions of the slaves even more painful. Spend a few minutes reflecting on and praying for people who are suffering under unjust leaders and governments around the world; people who are denied basic human rights and freedoms. Then turn your thoughts to your own situation. Very few of us suffer literal slavery, but you might feel trapped by some situation in your life such as pressured work conditions, family problems, money difficulties or some internal struggle. Ask God to release you from that slavery… to set you free from whatever chains you feel bound by… free to worship him.

---

### 3 Moment of release

*During the night Pharaoh summoned Moses and Aaron and said, 'Up! Leave my people, you and the Israelites! Go, worship the LORD as you have requested. Take your flocks and herds, as you have said, and go … '* (Exodus 12:31,32).

When the moment of release happened, it came very quickly, in the middle of the night. The Egyptians were scared and wanted to get rid of the Israelites as soon as possible. Moments of release can happen like that sometimes. Suddenly everything changes!

Pray about some hopeless situations you know about, asking God for breakthrough, release… Then, when you are ready, run or walk more urgently on this section of the path, imagining that you are escaping Egypt after many years of captivity, desperate to get away before the Egyptians change their minds.

### 4 Guided by God

*By day the LORD went ahead of them in a pillar of cloud to guide them on their way and by night in a pillar of fire to give them light, so that they could travel by day or night* (Exodus 13:21).

It must have been an amazing experience for the Israelites – literally able to see God guiding them every step of the way in cloud and fire. God guides us, too, in many different ways. But often the guidance we experience is more subtle than the cloud and fire of the Exodus. And sometimes we get confused about the right way to turn.

Pray about any decisions you are facing – big or small. Pray that you will make right choices. Pray for others you know are also facing decisions, that they will hear God clearly and follow him.

### 5 Provided by God

*The Israelites said to them [Moses and Aaron], 'If only we had died by the LORD's hand in Egypt! There we sat round pots of meat and ate all the food we wanted, but you have brought us out into this desert to starve this entire assembly to death.' Then the LORD said to Moses, 'I will rain down bread from heaven for you. The people are to go out each day and gather enough for that day* (Exodus 16:3,4).

Look around you at any growing things you can see… plants, trees, shrubs, birds… and thank God for those signs of life. We live in a land of plenty, not a desert; most of us have never experienced famine or shortage of food. Our food comes in packets and tins and sometimes it's hard to remember that we rely on harvests and farmers thousands of miles away.

Pray for good harvests this year, especially in lands prone to famine. Thank God for some of the foods you especially appreciate, and resolve not to take all you have for granted.

### 6 Refreshed by God

*. . . They camped at Rephidim, but there was no water for the people to drink … Then Moses cried out to the LORD, 'What am I to do with these people? They are almost ready to stone me.' The LORD answered Moses, '… take in your hand the staff with which you struck the Nile, and go. I will stand there before you by the rock at Horeb. Strike the rock, and water will come out of it for the people to drink'* (from Exodus 17:1–6).

Water is not only one of the necessities of life, but also a symbol of refreshment – spiritual refreshment as well as physical refreshment.

Talk to God about some of those areas of your life where you feel you particularly need refreshment. Then remember other people you know who might need that refreshment, too. Thank God that sometimes his refreshment comes in amazing and miraculous ways… even out of what looks like barren rock!

### 7 On the mountain

*When Moses came down from Mount Sinai with the two tablets of the Testimony in his hands, he was not aware that his face was radiant because he had spoken with the LORD… Afterwards all the Israelites came near him, and he gave them all the commands the LORD had given him on Mount Sinai* (from Exodus 34:29–32).

Have you ever had a 'mountain top' experience? A time when you felt that God was really close? Spend a few minutes remembering that experience now in as much detail as you can. Thank God that it happened. If you have never had a mountain top experience, then pray that God will bless you in that way.

## 8  Forgiven by God

*The people ... spoke against God and against Moses ... Then the L*ORD* sent venomous snakes among them; they bit the people and many Israelites died ... The L*ORD* said to Moses, 'Make a snake and put it up on a pole; anyone who is bitten can look at it and live'* (from Numbers 21:4–8).

Jesus used this incident to talk about himself being lifted up on the Cross, so *that everyone who believes in him may have eternal life* (John 3:15). Of course, neither the Cross nor the bronze snake would have been needed if no one had ever done wrong against God.

Now is your chance to apologise to God for anything you want to bring to him. Then imagine Jesus on the Cross, telling you that you are forgiven.

✂ — — — — — — — — — — — — — — — — — — — — — — — — — — — — — — — — — — — — —

## 9  Hesitating over the next step

*... 'Let us send men ahead to spy out the land for us and bring back a report about the route we are to take and the towns we will come to.' ... Taking with them some of the fruit of the land, they brought it down to us and reported, 'It is a good land that the L*ORD* our God is giving us.' But you were unwilling to go up ... 'The people are stronger and taller than we are; the cities are large, with walls up to the sky* (from Deuteronomy1:22–28).

The Israelites had nearly reached the Promised Land, and yet when the spies reported back they were scared of entering it. Because their fear was greater than their trust in God, they ended up wandering in the desert for 40 years.

We all suffer from fear of the unknown; perhaps especially fear of anything which might involve pain and suffering, either physical or emotional. Think about anything that frightens you about the future. Talk this through with God, and ask him to give you the courage to go forward, even when it is hard to take the next step.

✂ — — — — — — — — — — — — — — — — — — — — — — — — — — — — — — — — — — — — —

## 10  Journey's end

*After the death of Moses ... the L*ORD* said to Joshua son of Nun ... 'Now then, you and all these people, get ready to cross the Jordan River into the land I am about to give them – to the Israelites. I will give you every place where you set your foot, as I promised Moses'* (from Joshua 1:1–3).

No matter what difficult territory we go through on the way, no matter how tough the road or how scary the snakes, we are certainly heading for our Promised Land: heaven.

Spend a few minutes thinking about heaven. What can you remember Jesus saying about it? Then continue on your way, secure in the knowledge that this is your journey's destination.

✂ — — — — — — — — — — — — — — — — — — — — — — — — — — — — — — — — — — — — —

# The Elijah journey meditations

These are given here as they might be for photocopied signposts, but they could alternatively be recorded for listening to at each station.

---

### 1 Elijah's first appearance

*Now Elijah the Tishbite, from Tishbe in Gilead, said to Ahab, 'As the LORD, the God of Israel, lives, whom I serve, there will be neither dew nor rain in the next few years except at my word'* (1 Kings 17:1).

We never get a glimpse of the calling of Elijah, as we do for some other prophets. Yet, when he appears, he does so with a very strong message. There is going to be a drought and accompanying famine. This must have been a hard message for Elijah to give. Have there ever been times when you have had to give a hard message to someone? Or make a difficult phone call? Spend a few moments now, praying for people who have to give hard messages or bad news today – for example: police, doctors, businessmen and politicians.

---

### 2 Elijah fed by ravens

*Then the word of the LORD came to Elijah: 'Leave here, turn eastward and hide in the Kerith Ravine, east of the Jordan. You will drink from the brook, and I have ordered the ravens to feed you there'* (1 Kings 17:2–4).

Jesus taught us to pray, 'Give us this day our daily bread' – to ask God to provide for us physically and spiritually. Occasionally, this can happen in the most unexpected ways. I've never been fed by ravens, but I have been walking through the streets and suddenly seen an advert or a picture in a shop window, or heard a fragment of a song echoing through a stereo system – and God has spoken to me through these things.

Pray for yourself and your friends, that God would feed you today and that you would recognise his voice when he speaks, even if it's in unexpected ways.

---

### 3 Elijah received generously

*… When he came to the town gate, a widow was there gathering sticks. He called to her and asked, 'Would you bring me a little water in a jar so I may have a drink?' As she was going to get it, he called, 'And bring me, please, a piece of bread.'*

*… she replied, 'I don't have any bread – only a handful of flour in a jar and a little oil in a jug. I am gathering a few sticks to take home and make a meal for myself and my son, that we may eat it – and die'* (from 1 Kings 17:10–12).

Elijah asks the widow to make a small cake for him from the tiny amount she has, and he promises her that the jar of flour will not be used up nor the oil run dry until the rains come again. The widow trusts Elijah. She gives away part of her very last meal – but God provides miraculously for her!

I'm often amazed by her generosity and her trust in the stranger she meets by the town gate who might have just been spinning a tale to steal her food. I contrast it with my own mistrust of strangers and the difficulties I have at times balancing giving my time and my money with my own needs.

Think about times when you have shared yourself, your possessions, your talents or your time with others, and what has happened. Pray for wisdom – to know when to say 'yes' and when to say 'no' to the demands of others.

## 4 Elijah on Mount Carmel

*Elijah replied, '… You have abandoned the LORD's commands and have followed the Baals. Now summon the people from all over Israel to meet me on Mount Carmel. And bring the 450 prophets of Baal and the 400 prophets of Asherah … Elijah went before the people and said, 'How long will you waver between two opinions? If the LORD is God, follow him; but if Baal is God, follow him'* (1 Kings 18:18–21).

Elijah challenges the other prophets to prepare a sacrifice and call on their God to set fire to it.  Despite the prophets' dancing, shouting and slashing themselves, nothing happens to their sacrifice. In contrast, Elijah asks for water to be poured on his sacrifice to God before praying a simple prayer, at which God sends fire down from heaven to burn up the sacrifice. The people fall on their knees and cry, 'The Lord – he is God!'

Who are the false prophets in our society today? Who or what distracts us from serving God? Pray that you will learn to recognise the difference between the voice of God and all the other voices that compete for your attention. Pray for our society too; for all people with influence in our government; for those in the media. Pray that they would learn to listen to and follow God, rather than the contemporary equivalents of Baal, such as materialism, sex, power or celebrity status.

---

## 5 Elijah wants to die

*Elijah was afraid and ran for his life. When he came to Beersheba in Judah, he left his servant there, while he himself went a day's journey into the desert. He came to a broom tree, sat down under it and prayed that he might die. 'I have had enough, LORD,' he said. 'Take my life … '* (1 Kings 19:3,4).

There is something immensely comforting in knowing that even great prophets like Elijah suffered from depression! There is also something reassuring about the fact that God doesn't dismiss him or reprimand him for this; instead he lovingly provides for his most basic needs by sending an angel with food and drink, who coaxes him to eat, build up his strength and carry on.

Pray for any you know who are going through tough times… including yourself if that's you!

---

## 6 Elijah hears from God

*The LORD said, 'Go out and stand on the mountain in the presence of the LORD, for the LORD is about to pass by.'*

*Then a great and powerful wind tore the mountains apart … but the LORD was not in the wind. After the wind there was an earthquake, but the LORD was not in the earthquake. After the earthquake came a fire, but the LORD was not in the fire. And after the fire came a gentle whisper. When Elijah heard it, he pulled his cloak over his face and went out and stood at the mouth of the cave* (1 Kings 19:11–13).

Even though God can – and sometimes does – speak in amazing ways, most of the time he speaks in gentle whispers; whispers that, if we aren't careful, we can easily ignore.

Spend some time listening to God or simply sitting or standing in silence in God's presence. You might like to begin this time by praying the young prophet Samuel's simple prayer, 'Speak, Lord, your servant is listening.'

---

## 7 The call of Elijah's successor

*Elijah went up to him [Elisha] and threw his cloak around him. Elisha then left his oxen and ran after Elijah. 'Let me kiss my father and mother good-bye,' he said, 'and then I will come with you'* (from 1 Kings 19:19,20).

Elijah is told in his conversation on the mountain with God to call Elisha to succeed him as a prophet. When he is called, Elisha says goodbye not just to his parents; he says goodbye to his old lifestyle (completely slaughtering his oxen) to follow Elijah.

Pray for people making lifestyle changes at this moment: people moving town, or even moving country, to follow God's call; people who have to change jobs for whatever reason. Pray for them as they face the difficulties that starting again can bring.

### 8  Elijah sent to Ahab

*Then the word of the LORD came to Elijah the Tishbite: Go down to meet Ahab king of Israel, who rules in Samaria. He is now in Naboth's vineyard, where he has gone to take possession of it. Say to him, 'This is what the LORD says: Have you not murdered a man and seized his property?' Then say to him, 'This is what the LORD says: In the place where dogs licked up Naboth's blood, dogs will lick up your blood ...'* (from 1 Kings 21:17–19).

Once again Elijah has to deliver a terrible message from God. Ahab wants Naboth's vineyard but Naboth will not sell it to him. Then Ahab's wife Jezebel has Naboth framed and stoned for blasphemy so that Ahab can take possession of the land. Yet when Ahab hears these words from God through Elijah, he does mend his ways and wears sackcloth and ashes. Because of this, God spares him.

Pray for people who want to change their lifestyle but are finding it hard, particularly for those who are suffering from addictions or struggling with abusive or failing relationships.

- - - - - - - - - - - - - - - - - - - - - - - - - - - - - - - - - - - - - - - - -

### 9  Elisha's loyalty to Elijah

*When the LORD was about to take Elijah up to heaven in a whirlwind, Elijah and Elisha were on their way from Gilgal. Elijah said to Elisha, 'Stay here; the LORD has sent me to Bethel.'*

*But Elisha said, 'As surely as the LORD lives and as you live, I will not leave you'* (2 Kings 2:1,2).

Elisha was loyal and deeply devoted to Elijah. He wanted to stay with him to the very end, so when Elijah was called to various places he followed him faithfully, making the most of Elijah's remaining time.

Sometimes it's hard to say goodbye when we see friends move on to better things, or when we have to leave a group or church ourselves. And then there is the most devastating separation of all: death.

Pray for people who know that they have to say goodbye to someone soon, especially those who are close to someone who is dying.

- - - - - - - - - - - - - - - - - - - - - - - - - - - - - - - - - - - - - - - - -

### 10  Elijah at his journey's end, Elisha left behind

*As they were walking along and talking together, suddenly a chariot of fire and horses of fire appeared and separated the two of them, and Elijah went up to heaven in a whirlwind.*

*... [Elisha] picked up the cloak that had fallen from Elijah and ... struck the water with it. 'Where now is the LORD, the God of Elijah?' he asked. When he struck the water, it divided to the right and to the left, and he crossed over* (from 2 Kings 2:11–14).

Elijah finally reaches his destination, heaven, after all he has suffered on his long journey. Yet Elisha finds it hard to be left behind. He asks, 'Where is God?' And God shows him – not in words, but in actions, by parting the waters for him.

Ask God to bring to mind the people God wants you to show his love to. How can you best demonstrate his love to them? Ask God to give you his love to give away. Finally, give thanks for all the people who have demonstrated God's love to you over the years.

# Bible verses index

| Reference | Activity | Number |
|---|---|---|
| Mark 4:35–41 | Boats | 16 |
| Mark 4:35–41 | The calming of the storm | 41 |
| Mark 6:30–44 | House plan | 38 |
| Mark 6:30–34,3–56 | Treasuring the questions | 29 |
| Mark 11:12–14,21 | Bark | 36 |
| Mark 15 | Connections web | 25 |
| Luke 1 | Connections web | 25 |
| Luke 5:8,10 | A dramatic meal | 21 |
| Luke 5:17–25 | House plan | 38 |
| Luke 9:54 | A dramatic meal | 21 |
| Luke 10:38–41 | A dramatic meal | 21 |
| Luke 10:38–42 | House plan | 38 |
| Luke 22:39–46 | Holy week smell trail | 48 |
| Luke 22:45 | House plan | 38 |
| Luke 22:54–62 | Holy week smell trail | 58 |
| Luke 23:33–46 | Holy week smell trail | 48 |
| John 1 | Connections web | 25 |
| John 1:40 | A dramatic meal | 21 |
| John 2:1–11 | House plan | 38 |
| John 3:15 | The Exodus journey | 49 |
| John 4:13,14 | Fire and water | 43 |
| John 6:9 | A dramatic meal | 21 |
| John 6:48 | Walking the Bible | 32 |
| John 7:37–39 | Fire and water | 43 |
| John 8 | Connections web | 25 |
| John 8:1–11 | Sand confession | 5 |
| John 10:30 | Trinity hand symbol | 22 |
| John 10:38 | Trinity hand symbol | 22 |
| John 11 | A dramatic meal | 21 |
| John 11:17–44 | Multi-Sensory Gospels | 44 |
| John 11:20 | A dramatic meal | 21 |
| John 11:26 | Chewing things over | 24 |
| John 11:32 | A dramatic meal | 21 |
| John 12:1–8 | Holy week smell trail | 48 |
| John 12:4–6,10,22 | A dramatic meal | 21 |

| Reference | Activity | Number |
|---|---|---|
| John 13:1–15 | Holy week smell trail | 48 |
| John 14:2 | House plan | 38 |
| John 14:5 | A dramatic meal | 21 |
| John 14:6 | Walking the Bible | 32 |
| John 15:5 | Bark | 36 |
| John 15:5 | Chewing things over | 24 |
| John 16:7 | Trinity hand symbol | 22 |
| John 18:10 | A dramatic meal | 21 |
| John 19:38–42 | Holy week smell trail | 48 |
| John 20:22,23 | Padlock | 35 |
| John 20:22 | Feathers | 47 |
| John 20:24–29 | A dramatic meal | 21 |
| John 21:1–14 | Holy Week smell trail | 48 |
| Acts 2:1–4 | Fire and water | 43 |
| Acts 2:2–4 | Feathers | 47 |
| Acts 10:9–16 | Labels | 17 |
| Acts 12 | Connections web | 25 |
| Romans 8 | Abstract art Bible pictures | 30 |
| 1 Corinthians 11:26 | Bread prayers | 15 |
| 1 Corinthians 12:12–31 | Pipe cleaners | 19 |
| 2 Corinthians 3:17 | Trinity hand symbol | 22 |
| Galatians 5:13–25 | Fruits of the Spirit installations | 27 |
| Galatians 6:7 | Thistles | 8 |
| 1 Timothy 2:1–8 | Wallet prayers | 14 |
| Titus 3:3–7 | Dissolving | 2 |
| Titus 3:3–7 | Wiping the slate clean | 3 |
| Hebrews 6:13–20 | Anchor of hope | 40 |
| 1 Peter 1:1,2 | Trinity hand symbol | 22 |
| Revelation 6:9,10 | Scrapping injustice | 12 |
| Revelation 21:1–4 | Scrapping injustice | 12 |
| Revelation 22:1,2 | Bark | 36 |
| Any passage | Quote cards | 28 |
| Any passage | Treasuring the questions | 29 |
| Any passage | Abstract art Bible pictures | 30 |
| Any passage | Walking the Bible | 32 |

# Group size index

**Recommended for small groups – up to 20 people:**
Activities 1, 2, 5, 6, 13, 21, 25, 26, 28, 31, 32, 33, 39

**Recommended for groups of up to 60 people:**
Activities 3, 7, 10, 15, 16, 29, 35, 36, 38, 40, 46, 47, 48

**Suitable for any size of group:**
Activities 4, 8, 9, 11, 12, 14, 17, 18, 19, 20, 23, 24, 27, 30, 34, 37, 29, 41, 42, 43, 44, 45, 49, 50

# Other books in the Multi-Sensory series

✳ **fresh**   ✳ **innovative**   ✳ **imaginative**   ✳ **inspirational**   ✳ **practical**

## MULTI-SENSORY CHURCH

Over 30 ready-to-use ideas for creative churches and small groups

**Sue Wallace**

This invaluable resource includes a variety of ways of exploring the senses to expand your understanding and grow your delight in prayer, liturgy, Bible reading, celebration, labyrinths and much more.

## MULTI-SENSORY PRAYER

Over 60 ready-to-use ideas for creative churches and small groups

**Sue Wallace**

Ways to use the senses to enrich your prayer experience – using everything from candles and broken pottery to nuts, leaves, newspapers, dough and mirrors!

## MULTI-SENSORY TOGETHER

15 ready-to-use sessions for Bible exploration in creative small groups

**Ian Birkinshaw**

15 complete sessions for leaders will breathe new life into small group Bible study experience. Will appeal to a range of learning styles. Based on a range of Biblical material from both Old and New Testaments.

## MULTI-SENSORY SEASONS

15 ready-to-use Bible-based sessions through the seasons for creative small groups

**Wendy Rayner and Annie Slade**

15 complete small group sessions based on a range of Biblical material from both Old and New Testaments with sessions that can be used any time or tied to a specific season of the church calendar.

---

This series is just part of a wide range of resources for churches and small groups published by Scripture Union. There's also a free online magazine about the world of small groups called church@home. Go to
**www.scriptureunion.org.uk/churchathome**

SU publications are available from Christian bookshops, on the Internet or via mail order. You can:

**phone** SU's mail order line: 0845 0706006

**email** info@scriptureunion.org.uk

**fax** 01908 856020

**log on** to www.scriptureunion.org.uk

**write** to SU Mail Order, PO Box 5148, Milton Keynes MLO, MK2 2YX